Literary History:
Theory and Practice

D1219742

Literary History: Theory and Practice

*Proceedings of
the Northeastern
University
Center for
Literary Studies*

Vol. 2, 1984

*Herbert L. Sussman
Editor*

Department of English, Northeastern University
360 Huntington Avenue, Boston, Massachusetts 02115

Distributed by Northeastern University Press
17 Cushing Hall
360 Huntington Avenue, Boston, Massachusetts 02115

Literary History.

(Proceedings of the Northeastern University Center for Literary
Studies; vol. 2)
Proceedings of three symposia held at Northeasten University in 1983-
1984 by the Northeastern University Center for Literary Studies.
1. Literature—History and criticism—Theory, etc.—Congresses.
I. Northeastern University (Boston, Mass.). Center for Literary Studies.
II. Series.
PN441.L485 1984   801'.95   84-42935
ISBN 0-930350-73-1

Table of Contents

Preface

In 1983-1984 the Northeastern University Center for Literary Studies considered the topic "Literary History: Theory and Practice." The speakers at the three symposia held at Northeastern University during that year were Professors Sandra Gilbert, Department of English, University of California, Davis, and Susan Gubar, Department of English, Indiana University; Jeffrey Mehlman, Department of Modern Languages, Boston University; and Lawrence Lipking, Department of English, Northwestern University. Professor Bonnie Costello, Department of English, Boston University, responded to Professors Gilbert and Gubar; Professor Naomi Schor, Department of French, Brown University, responded to Professor Mehlman; and Ruth Whitman, Radcliffe College/Harvard University responded to Professor Lipking.

The hope of the Center in selecting this topic was to explore the practice of literary history at this particular moment in critical discourse, a moment when theory claims that literary history, like all forms of history, is best seen as a collection of narratives, as a set of fictions constructed from particular interpretive viewpoints. As

Lawrence Lipking notes, "All literary history, we hear these days, consists of stories." And yet, as the talks and responses collected in this volume suggest, notwithstanding the claims of theory, the writing of literary history continues to be an urgent and vital enterprise. Whether the enterprise calls for a revision of the idea of modernism in order to include the movement's opposition to the middle-class woman writer, or urges us to see the repressed political context of certain fiction and deconstructionist criticism in twentieth-century France, or charts continuity and change in poetic style from Homer through the Romantics, the literary historians in this volume assume the necessity and responsibility of continuously recasting our sense of the literary past. All seem to share the belief, articulated by Lipking, that although literary history may consist of "stories," "not all tales are the same. Some stories work better than others."

In addition to thanking our speakers and respondents, the Center for Literary Studies Committee wishes to thank President Kenneth Ryder, Dean Richard Astro and those other members of the faculty and staff through whose support and efforts the work of the Center has been accomplished. We would also like to thank Suzanne Sowinski for her help in preparing this volume.

Center for Literary Studies Committee

Herbert L.Sussman, Chairperson
Francis Blessington
Irene R. Fairley
Stuart Peterfreund
Kinley E. Roby

Sandra M. Gilbert
Susan Gubar

Tradition and the Female Talent

Towards the end of the eighteenth century a change came about which, if I were re-writing history, I should describe more fully and think of greater importance than the Crusades or the Wars of the Roses. The middle-class woman began to write.
—Virginia Woolf, *A Room of One's Own*

In the nineteenth century men were confident, the women were not but in the twentieth century the men have no confidence.
—Dashiell Hammett to Gertrude Stein, in *Everybody's Autobiography*

The existing monuments form an ideal order among themselves, which is modified by the introduction of the new (the really new) work of art among them.
—T.S. Eliot, "Tradition and the Individual Talent"

On December 30, 1927, Max Beerbohm wrote Virginia Woolf a strangely ambiguous fan letter. Praising her criticism for its likeness to her father's work—"if he had been a 'Georgian' and a woman, just so would he have written"—he went on quite unexpectedly to attack her fiction: "Your novels beat me—black and blue. I retire howling, aching, sore; full, moreover, of an acute sense of disgrace. I return later, I re-submit myself to the discipline. No use: I am carried out half-dead."[1] What was bothering the incomparable Max? Certainly, in the context of his admiration for *The Common Reader*, his somewhat paranoid association of Woolf's novels with bondage and discipline seems inexplicable, almost bizarre.

To be sure, Beerbohm goes on in the same letter to provide an explanation of his pain which would appear to suggest that his quarrel with Leslie Stephen's daughter is part of a larger generational conflict in the world of letters. "I don't really, insidious though you are, believe in your Cambridge argument that a new spirit exacts a new method of narration," he explains, identifying himself with "Homer's and Thackeray's method, and Tolstoy's and Tom's, Dick's, and Chaucer's, Maupassant's and Harry's," all presumably methods grounded in the modes and manners of traditional realism. Thus he sets himself, as a late-Victorian man of letters, against Woolf, as a representative of Cambridge/ Bloomsbury modernism. Despite this explanation, however, Beerbohm's description of the effect Woolf's novels have on him, together with his list of the Toms, Dicks, and Harrys who constitute his literary patrilineage, implies that more than a conflict of cohorts is being enacted here. Curiously enough, moreover, the rhetoric of his letter echoes a story he had published seven years earlier, a story about a literary battle not between the generations but between the sexes. Indeed, Beerbohm's image of a generational struggle masks a more profound sexual-literary struggle dramatized not only in his fiction but also in the fiction of many of his contemporaries.

"The Crime," which was included in Beerbohm's *And Even Now*, describes the acute "sense of disgrace" experienced by a nameless narrator who impetuously flings a woman writer's novel into a fireplace but cannot seem to burn the book up. Vacationing in a rented cottage in a remote county, this lonely man of letters compares himself at the outset of the story to "Lear in the hovel on the heath."[2] Idly looking for something to read, he picks up the latest novel by a well-known woman writer whom he has met and been daunted by on several occasions: "She had...a sisterly, brotherly way....But I was conscious that my best, under her eye, was not good...she said for me just what I had tried to say, and proceeded to show me just why it was wrong" (247). In fact, he reminisces, his few conversations with her led him to speculate on the "'sex war,'" that "we are often told, is to be one of the features of the world's future—women demanding the right to do men's work and men refusing, resisting, counter-attacking" (248). While he claims that he himself has never had his "sense of fitness jarred; nor a spark of animosity roused" by most feminist demands, he confesses that he is disturbed by the idea of a woman practicing the art of writing. More specifically, he admits that he is bothered if a woman is "an habitual, professional author, with a passion for her art, and a fountain-pen and an agent, and sums down in advance of royalties on sales in Canada and Australia..." (248-49).

But the novelist whose book Beerbohm's man of letters picks up in his country cottage is emphatically all these things and, worse still, her work, as its jacket copy suggests, is characterized by "immense and intense vitality"; her newest novel, say the critics, is "a book that will live" (247). Furthermore, when he begins reading this book, he soon discovers that the novel is itself a *Kunstlerroman* about a successful woman of letters, a mother who sits "writing in a summer-house at the e'nd of a small garden," her pen travelling "rapidly across the foolscap" (249). It is no wonder, then, that he feels "exquisite satisfaction" when he discovers that, following "an impulse...almost before I was conscious of it" (250), he has committed the heinous crime of flinging his landlord's copy of this woman's book into the fire, where it stands for a moment gloriously glowing. But although at first "little tongues of bright colour" (251) leaping from the binding let him exult that "I had scored...perfectly" against this "Poor woman!," he soon discovers to his dismay that the text itself refuses to be burnt. Enacting a cross between a ritual rape and a sacrificial burning at the stake, this increasingly obsessed narrator "rakes" the book "fore and aft" with a poker, "carve[s]" it into sections, "subdivide[s] it, spread[s] it, redistribute[s] it" (251-52). Yet still its intense and immense vitality proclaims that "it [is] a book that will live—do what one might" (252). Finally, therefore, Beerbohm's disgraced man of letters has to concede that his female antagonist has "scored again." Not only has he been unable to destroy her book in "the yawning crimson jaws" of his hearth, her book has itself damped his flames. As his fire goes out (252), he is left alone in a small and chilly room, as dispossessed as a parodic Lear confined to the prison of his consciousness.

Beerbohm's story is, of course, a masterfully comical satire on the futile rage with which men of letters greeted female literary achievement. At the same time, however, it is also, as the author's own letter to Virginia Woolf suggests, an enactment of that futile rage. What the juxtaposition of the letter and story suggests, therefore, is that the existence of a tradition of "habitual, professional" women authors made for a battle of the sexes over the province and provenance of literature, a battle which men, rightly or wrongly, felt they were losing in the years when Beerbohm wrote.

Not surprisingly, the author of *Zuleika Dobson* (1906), that ultimate comedy of the *femme fatale*, was no non-combatant in the war between men and women that had been gathering force since the late 19th century. Always masking his masculinist anxieties with elegant irony, Beerbohm nevertheless understood the deeply dialectic relationship in which men and women found themselves by the *fin de siècle*, a relationship that, as Virginia Woolf herself pointed out, was historically unprecedented.

Eight years after Beerbohm wrote "The Crime," after all, she observes in a passage from *A Room of One's Own* that we have used as an epigraph here that "toward the end of the 18th century a change came about which, if I were rewriting history, I should describe more fully and think of greater importance than the Crusades or the War of the Roses. The middle-class woman began to write" (68). Earlier, moreover, in just the year when Beerbohm wrote "The Crime," Woolf had analyzed the empowering implications of the entrance of women into literary history, noting in a letter to *The New Statesman* that "the 17th century produced more remarkable women than the 16th. The 18th than the 17th, and the 19th than all three put together.... When I compare the Duchess of Newcastle with Jane Austen, the matchless Orinda with Emily Brontë, Mrs. Haywood with George Eliot, Aphra Behn with Charlotte Brontë, the advance in intellectual power seems to me not only sensible but immense."[3] Describing the evolution of a tradition of immense and intense vitality, Woolf's statement almost seems to gloss the dilemma Beerbohm dramatizes in "The Crime." Moreover, the implicit dialogue between Beerbohm and Woolf that we have traced here seems itself to gloss the asymmetrical response of literary men and literary women to the strong new presence of women in the literary marketplace. For, as we shall argue throughout this essay, when the middle-class woman began not only to enter the professions but specifically to enter the profession of letters, both sexes reacted with powerful but powerfully different changes in their views of the world and themselves. To begin with and most dramatically, male writers like James in America and Wilde in England could not help noticing that theirs was among the earliest generations to have female precursors. But what did it mean for such men to have to confront not only the commercial success of, say, Harriet Beecher Stowe in America and Mary Elizabeth Braddon in England, but also the cultural achievement of, say, George Eliot, Elizabeth Browning and Charlotte Brontë in England?

As we shall show, the historical change was disquieting for them because it had several ramifications: first, because women's new autonomy smashed the Oedipal paradigm in which the mother represents a figure who is to be possessed rather than self-possessed, the change suggested, as Ann Douglas has demonstrated, a frightening feminization of culture,[4] an emasculating engulfment by the mother; second, and perhaps even more important, because for late 19th- and early 20th-century literary sons the Oedipal struggle to take the place and the possession of the father was now in some sense doomed from the start, this historical change reinforced the sense of belatedness— the anxiety about the originary power of the father—upon which, as Harold Bloom has shown, literary men had already been brooding for several centuries. What Matthew Arnold defined as "this strange disease of modern life" became a dis-ease with what

James's Basil Ransom called in *The Bostonians* "a feminine, chattering, canting age."[5] At the same time, however, the very dis-ease fostered by this unprecedented cultural crisis worked paradoxically to the advantage of many literary men. For as the richness of the (male) modernist tradition attests and as we shall argue later, for many male writers Beerbohm's futile rage became fertile rage, fueling the innovations of the *avant garde* in order to ward off the onslaughts of women.

* * * * *

Recently, casually, and almost comically, Harold Bloom declared that "the first true breach with literary continuity will be brought about in generations to come if the burgeoning religion of Liberated Woman spreads from its clusters of enthusiasts to dominate the West. Homer will cease to be the inevitable precursor and the rhetoric and forms of our literature then may break at last from tradition."[6] Bloom seems to be speculating provisionally about some future catastrophe, yet it is possible to argue that what he describes in such ironically apocalyptic terms is an event that has already occurred. Certainly, his remarks appear to gloss a novella that the young Aldous Huxley published in the same year that Max Beerbohm published "The Crime." "The Farcical History of Richard Greenow" was the lead work in a volume with the resonantly and resolutely nihilistic title *Limbo*, and in keeping with such nihilism Huxley's tale traced the misadventures and growing misogyny of a literary man who lives out in his own person the living end of masculine history that Bloom describes.

Dick Greenow, the anti-hero of Huxley's farcical *Kunstlerroman*, starts as a sensitive boy with a domineering younger sister named Millicent, whose dollhouse fascinates him, although, as if she had already read Ibsen, "it simply didn't interest her."[7] Enduring the standard late Victorian male education, first at a public school called Aesop and then at Cantaloup College, Oxford, he falls hopelessly in love at the age of 16 with one Francis Quarles, a handsome incarnation of classical literary history who inspires him to fits of sentimental verse-writing from which he is luckily awakened by a sudden sense that he had been "suffering from anemia of the brain" (23). Later, at college, he dedicates himself to "all that [is] most intellectually distinguished" (29), but soon unnervingly discovers that he has been possessed by the spirit of a female novelist named "Pearl Bellairs," who takes over his body to write long, saccharine romances while he is asleep. "Her" first work is entitled *Heartsease Fitzroy: The Story of a Young Girl* and, ironically enough, its instant success helps finance his "unproductive male labours" (38). After going down from college "in a blaze of glory," therefore, Dick pragmatically continues his dual career. While he works on his *New Synthetic Philosophy*, Pearl indefatigably completes *La Belle Dame Sans Morality* and *Daisy's Voyage to Cytherea*, along with a series of articles "for the girls of Britain" (49). But, as Dick gradually loses his intellectual potency and becomes little Dick, Pearl (with her fanciful belle airs) increasingly manifests herself as the belle heir, a 20th-century inheritor of the women's tradition founded by such precursors as *Jane Eyre*. Worse still, as his writing becomes increasingly elitist and occult, her work, inspired by his readings of George Sand, Elizabeth Barrett Browning, and Mrs. Humphrey Ward, becomes ever more powerful and popular.

The crisis of Dick's life, which seems to parody an intensified historical crisis for literary men, comes with the advent of World War I. As he travels toward London, planning to become a conscientious objector, even the wheels of the train "refus[e] to recite Milton," as if prophetically warning him about the demise of the cultural history he had hoped to inherit. Finally, moreover, his experiences during the war document that demise, for while his sister Millicent supervises 300 clerks at the Ministry of Munitions with "unsurpassed efficiency" (95), Pearl writes jingoistic propaganda for the "Women of England." Distraught about the "horrible Bluebeard's chamber of his own brain" (67), Dick visits a psychiatrist whose word association test elicits a response which seems to offer some solution to the mystery of his schizophrenic seizures, for the word "woman" seems to lead inexorably to the word "novelist" (67). Though Dick continues to stage dramatic anti-war protests as an intellectual socialist/pacifist, therefore, he slowly sinks into madness, with Pearl demonically possessing his brain and pen. By the end of the war, when she is strong enough to emerge and register to vote, he is confined as a lunatic and force-fed the way the suffragists had been. Filled with revulsion at Pearl's proliferating vulgarity, he desperately tries to will his body to science, but even here she intervenes, wresting the pen from him and begging to be buried "in a little country church-yard with little marble angels." In the end, his last desperate scribblings, the fragments he has tried to shore against his ruin, are "thrown away as being merely the written ravings of a madman" (115).

To be sure, despite the desolation of Dick's fate, Huxley's story is as farcical as its title indicates; like Beerbohm's it seems to have been intended as a deliciously sardonic diversion. As Huxley himself indicates in the text, moreover, he is creating a comedy of doubles like Jekyll/Hyde in fiction, William Sharp and Fiona McLeod in real life. Nevertheless, it seems significant that Richard Greenow emerges as a prototypically modern alienated intellectual specifically within the context of a tale depicting degrading femininity let loose in a culture where the apocalypse Bloom described was already taking place. For little Dick Greenow does seem to be the apothesis of a *poèt maudit* and he seems to have become such a figure precisely because of the excursions of his sister, Millicent, and the incursions of her double, Pearl. At the same time, their assaults upon his integrity seem to have been made possible by the intellectual and moral impoverishment, the historical weariness, of great male centers of learning like Aesop and Cantaloup.

That Huxley and Beerbohm were not alone in their sense of a literary apocalypse set in motion by the changing relations of the sexes to modes of literary production is further suggested by the work of Henry James. His famous "The Death of the Lion," for instance, counterpoints the ignominious demise of a truly great man of letters and the horrifying rise of two vulgarly popular literary transsexuals,[8] while his "The Next Time" traces another male literary fall associated with a female literary rise, specifically the fall of a novelist who fails to descend to the level of what would be commercially successful in an age of "trash triumphant" (245) and the rise of a woman writer who produces voluminous bestsellers with the greatest of ease. Similarly, James's "Greville Fane" portrays the "imperturbable industry" of a woman novelist "who could invent stories by the yard but couldn't write a page of English" (155). Although James's narrator is in many ways sympathetic to this "dull kind woman" who has been, as he shows, ruthlessly exploited by her children, he condescingly explains that he "liked her" because "she rested me so from literature," which was to him "an irritation, a torment" (154). His sense of his own "admirably absolute" failure, in other words, is set against his vision of the Ouida-like Greville Fane as "an old sausage-mill" giving forth "any poor verbal scrap that had been dropped into her" (156) and receiving lucrative rewards for such vigorous banality. In all three of these James tales, then, the male writer is rarified, marginalized, and impoverished, while the female writer, like Beerbohm's woman novelist and Huxley's Pearl Bellairs, achieves an "immense vitality" and a sinister centrality.

Historically speaking, which figure comes first, the neurasthenic man of letters or the imaginative female romancer? Does Pearl Bellairs gain her strength from Dick's weakness or is Dick weakened by her strength? Huxley's story, like James's tales, emphasizes the second of these alternatives while not discounting the first. To begin with, after all, Dick Greenow is certainly not a powerful heir of his patrilineage, but his physical fragility and mental effeminacy are matched by, say, the bovine stupidity of the supposedly powerful Francis Quarles. Because neither of these men can be an inheritor, culture inevitably falls into the hands of Pearl and Millicent. But increasingly, as the story progresses, these two female demons of efficiency become themselves the causes of Dick's diminution. Like Beerbohm's woman writer, who says for the narrator "just what [he] had tried to say" and then proceeds "to show [him] why it [is] wrong" (247), Pearl usurps even Dick's language, as she invades "the sanctities of his private life" and tramples "on his dearest convictions, denying his faith" (62). As the novella goes on, indeed, Huxley uses the rhetoric of parasitism and vampirism to describe Pearl's insistent and untiring appropriation of Dick's body: she is "greedy for life" (71); "watching perpetually like a hungry tigress for her opportunity," she takes "possession of his conscious faculties" so that he is "lost, blotted off the register of living souls while she [performs] with intense and hideous industry, her self-appointed task" (73-74). Like Zuleika Dobson, she is a *femme fatale* whose voracity requires the suicide of the literary man; like those of Beerbohm's woman of letters—or, indeed, those of his Virginia Woolf—her "insidious" ways utterly destroy the male and the culture he represents; like those of James's imaginative women, her fantasies cripple man's fancy, and her "hideous industry" and "immense vitality" leave him with "an acute sense of disgrace."

Given the vampiric and parasitic qualities of this paradigmatic literary woman, one cannot help thinking that she seems uncannily like a female prototype Thomas Hardy once created: his famous 1898 "Ivy Wife." Looking for a host to feed on, Hardy's vegetable *femme fatale* tries first "to love a full-boughed beech/And be as high as he," then to give "the grasp of partnership" to a plane tree, but finally in her "affection" she strives "to coll an ash," who "in trust" receives her love.[9] But that the ash accepts her embrace, as the other trees do not, implies, in terms of the question we have been raising here, that some secret death-wish, some ashen neurasthenia, is in fact a precondition for female triumph. And certainly the victory of the Ivy Wife is in some ways significantly analogous to the triumphs of Pearl Bellairs and her fictive sisters, for, as she tells us, "with my soft green claw/I cramped and bound him as I wove.../Such was my love: ha-ha!" After all, like Pearl and the others, she is a tenaciously successful parasite, cramping her host's style with what appears to be her virtue but is really her "hideous industry." Worse still, her exhilarated assertion—"Such was my love: ha-ha!"—expresses the alien urgency of female desire, with its threat to male potency.

Perhaps more than his modernist successors, however, Hardy feels free to imagine a punitive plot in which his Ivy Wife is destroyed by her own aspirations.

> But in my triumph I lost sight of afterhaps. Soon he
>   Being bark-bound, flagged, snapped, fell outright,
>   And in his fall felled me!

While this may in some sense be the story of Pearl Bellairs, it is emphatically not that of Beerbohm's or James's women (and even Pearl Bellairs will, after all, live on through her amazingly successful writing). No doubt because Hardy still feels himself hardily embedded in the sexual conventions of Victorian culture, he is able to annihilate his overreaching female Faust. Yet he does also have to kill the male host along with the female guest, and the anxious ambiguities his poem enacts therefore point to a story he published in 1893, a story about an "Ivy Wife" which provides a significant background to the struggles over literary primacy that we have been tracing here.

Hardy's "An Imaginative Woman," which was included in *Life's Little Ironies*, dramatizes the increasing infatuation of a would-be poet named Ella Marchmill, who seems in her female submissiveness like a paradigmatic *elle*, with a true poet who has the appropriate name of Robert Trewe. The only daughter of a struggling man of letters and the wife of a "commonplace" small-arms manufacturer, Ella publishes what Hardy makes quite clear is second-rate verse under the pseudonym of John Ivy, and an Ivy Wife is what, metaphorically speaking, she becomes in her relationship both to her husband and to the fantasy lover/double into which she transforms Robert Trewe. For though the most striking irony in this tale of one of life's little ironies is that Ella never actually meets Trewe, she becomes obsessed with him when she and her family rent his rooms in a seaside resort for a month one summer. A poem of his, Ella recalls, had appeared in large type at the top of a page in a magazine on which her own poem about the same subject was published in small type at the bottom. He had then assembled his poems in a volume that sold successfully, but when she tried to follow his example her own collection had fallen "dead in a fortnight—if it had ever been alive."[10] For some time, indeed, "with sad and hopeless envy Ella Marchmill had often and often scanned the rival poet's work, so much stronger as it always was than her own feeble lines. She had imitated him, and her inability to touch his level would send her into fits of despondency" (9).

No wonder, then, that when she finds herself actually inhabiting Trewe's room she feverishly studies the relics of identity he has left behind. Possessed by the Ivy Wife's passion to "be as high as he," she dons his macintosh and hat, imagining his coat as "the mantle of Elijah" and praying "would it might inspire me to rival him, glorious genius that he is!" (12). But although "*His* heart had beat inside that coat and *his* brain had worked under that hat," her "weakness beside him [makes] her feel quite sick" (13). Similarly, when she finds his picture secreted behind a photograph of the royal family, she studies his "striking countenance" adoringly (16) but soon confesses that "It's *you* who've so cruelly eclipsed me these many times!" (17). Finally, and most dramatically, she scans "the half-obliterated pencillings on the wall-paper" next to his bed (17), perceiving "the least of them" as "so palpitating, that it seemed as if his very breath...fanned her cheeks from those walls" (17). Enclosed by the ghostly traces of Trewe's script, she voraciously invokes his presence, imagining that "she was sleeping on a poet's lips, immersed in the very essence of him, permeated by his spirit as by an ether" (18). In a number of ways, then, she seems as vulnerable, passive, and secondary as the Ivy Wife. Disciple to master, student to teacher, even Danäe to Zeus, Mary to Holy Spirit, "permeated" by male authority, she appears more threatened than threat.

Yet, oddly enough, while Ella continues humbly to hope for a meeting with this deific man of letters, the distant Trewe responds with cursory civility to the letters she writes him as "John Ivy" and misses a meeting she has arranged. Trewe, it appears, has gone into a bizarre decline which we soon learn is not unrelated to his new volume of verse, *Lyrics to a Woman Unknown*, a book whose impetus is a mysterious passion for a kind of *Ferne Geliebte*, an "imaginary woman alone," for—he himself insists—"in spite of what has been said in some quarters" there is "no real woman behind the title" (26). Soon, we learn that he has actually committed suicide and that he has done so because of this "imaginary woman." On the one hand, therefore, Trewe appears to have been sapped of strength because there was no mother, sister, or female friend "tenderly devoted" to him (26); on the other hand, although he says "there is no real woman" behind the title of his newest volume, the "imaginary woman" whose absence triggers his death seems suspiciously related to the "imaginative woman" named Ella Marchmill. To make matters worse, moreover, although Ella is genuinely distraught at Trewe's demise, she soon, in what Hardy insinuates is another one of life's little ironies, gives birth to the poet's successor, a son who "by an inexplicable trick of Nature" (32) looks uncannily like this man she has never seen.

To be sure, she herself dies in labor, confessing to her husband that she has been mysteriously "possessed" (31), but in fact her production of this apparently illegitimate child suggests that she has radically subverted the very patrilineage which refused to acknowledge her poetry, for, by creating an alien heir to literary tradition, she has triumphed over both Trewe and her husband, supplanting the one and undermining the other. Like the Ivy Wife in other words, she "nurtures a love" which "cramp[s] and bind[s]" her male hosts, even though their "fall felled" her; and like Pearl Bellairs, she leaves a legacy of chaos which dramatically expresses her sense of herself as a second-rate poet and a second-rate person. For, at least subtextually, Hardy's language implies that Ella's ambition somehow causes the sexual frustration that kills Trewe, since the reality of the fiercely "imaginative" woman annihilates the dream of the nurturing "imaginary woman." Finally, then, and most ironically, Ella does not merely destroy Trewe; more terribly, she recreates him in diminished form as an effeminately vulnerable and potentially disenfranchised child. As early as 1893, then, Hardy was brooding on the very issues that Beerbohm, Huxley, and James were more ferociously and comically to dramatize.

* * * * *

The prominent turn-of-the-century authors whose stories we have reviewed here were not merely paranoid, for their fictions document the astonishing rise of commercially successful women of letters throughout the middle and late 19th century in England and America. The prototypes of such stereotypes as Huxley's Pearl Bellairs and James's Greville Fane were not only, after all, stellar figures like Harriet Beecher Stowe and Mary Elizabeth Braddon; they were part of what Hawthorne once called "a damned mob of scribbling women,"[11] a "mob" that had begun to invade the literary marketplace with alarming success and striking visibility as early as 1855, when Hawthorne made his defensive remark, and for several reasons the first impact of this invasion was felt in America by men like Hawthorne. Cut off not only from the long history of the English fatherland but also from the literary patrilineage that, drawing on a tradition from Chaucer and Shakespeare to Milton and the Romantics, endowed the man of letters with the powers of a priest or prophet, American artists felt emasculated and thus reacted to the achievement of women more quickly and with more virulent misogyny than their British contemporaries did. Indeed, it could be said that they began to create a myth of America as a country of aggressive women; expressing such a male sense of assault and invasion, one anonymous commentator complained in 1856 that "France, England, Germany, Sweden, but most of all our own country has furnished forth an army of women in the walks of literature...quite to the shame of manhood."[12] His feelings moreover, are confirmed by the fact that out of 558 poems published in the 1870s by the prestigious *Atlantic Monthly*, 201 were by women.[13] By 1896 the poet Louise Guiney felt confident enough about the poetic achievements of her sex to write that "The women over here are regular Atalantas in the poetic race."[14]

As for what Nina Baym has called "Woman's Fiction," and what Henry Nash Smith has defined as the scribbling woman's "cosmic success story," it is arguable that by the mid-19th century in America such a genre defined and dominated the literary marketplace.[15] Henry James, for instance, believed that "women, with their free use of leisure, were the chief consumers of novels and therefore were increasingly becoming producers of them. The feminine attitude, now disengaging itself from that of men, was in point of fact coming to be all that the novel was."[16] Commenting on the same phenomenon, the critic Thomas Beer observed that "...if you were a proper editor...you did not trifle with the Titaness and for her sake you issued tales of women, by women, for women...."[17] No wonder, then, that Edmund Clarence Stedman characterized this period in his American literature anthology as "the woman's age," and no wonder, either, that just a few years ago Leslie Fiedler in the *New York Times Book Review* described the 19th-century American "struggle of High Art and Low" as "a battle of the sexes" in which the serious male author was "condemned to neglect and poverty by a culture simultaneously commercialized and feminized."[18] Despite the special historical and social problems with which American literary men were confronted, however, their response to this "Woman's age" provided a crucial paradigm of what was to become an equally passionate anxiety on the other side of the Atlantic. For though it can be argued that at least in England a tradition of male feminism extends from Godwin and Shelley to Mill, Meredith, Gissing, and Shaw, the very existence of such a tradition suggests the unnerving centrality of the "woman question" in 19th-century Britain. By the *fin de siècle*, moreover, even the most seemingly supportive Englishmen were as nervous about female literary power as their American precursors.

Oscar Wilde, for instance, the son of a woman poet, the editor of *Woman's World*, and the author of an apparently celebratory essay on "English Poetesses," defended himself against the threat of female autonomy by annihilating the desirous daughter of Herodias in *Salome*. Furthermore, even while praising "the really remarkable awakening of woman's song that characterizes the latter half of our century in England,"[19] Wilde undercut his affirmation of English poetesses by singling out figures like "Eliza Haywood, who is immortalized by the badness of her work, and has a niche in *The Dunciad*" (107), "Mrs. Ratcliffe [sic], who introduced the romantic novel, and has consequently much to answer for" (108), and "poor L.E.L., whom Disraeli described in one of his...letters...as 'the personification of Brompton'" (108). In fact, Wilde's principal thesis is that the only great English poetess is Elizabeth Barrett Browning, with all the others being characterized essentially as versions of Ella Marchmill.

In thus defining and degrading "scribbling women" in an 1888 issue of England's *Queen*, Wilde would seem to have been doing exactly what such satirists as Bret Harte and Mark Twain had done earlier in America. Harte's "Miss Mix by Ch - l - tte Br - ntë" (1867) is a hilarious parody of *Jane Eyre* that the American humorist reinterprets as a melodramatic farce in which the smugly virtuous heroine leaves her childhood home at "Minerva Cottage" to enter the service (and the arms) of "Mr. Rawjester," the polygamous master of "Blunderbore Hall," who bears a "remarkable likeness to a gorilla."[20] As for Twain, one of the most comical characters in his

Huckleberry Finn (1885) is the lugubrious lyricist Emmeline Grangerford, whose "Ode to Stephen Dowling Bots, Dec'd" is merely one of the inadvertently humorous mortuary verses that she grinds out with fatal fluency: "...she could rattle off poetry like nothing," explains Huck. "She didn't ever have to stop to think."[21] Like Wilde's Eliza Haywood and Harte's "Ch - l - tte Br - ntë," Emmeline is "immortalized by the badness of her work" and, as we quickly discover, she was killed by her own eager vulgarity just as surely as she is buried by Twain's hilarious recounting of it, for "she pined away and did not live long" after the traumatic occasion when she "hung fire on a rhyme for [a] dead person's name, which was Whistler" (121).

To be sure what Harte and Twain offer are apparently light-hearted caricatures, and yet the motivating force behind their comedy—as behind the comedy of Huxley and Beerbohm—is precisely the sexual anxiety experienced by writers like Poe, Hawthorne, and Melville. It is not impossible either, however, that such sexual anxiety is what drew the modernist English novelist D.H. Lawrence to write about an unlikely subject for him—namely, the masters of the so-called American Renaissance. His *Studies in Classic American Literature* was, interestingly enough, the first major critical assessment of these artists, and though he does not emphasize the point, he may well have been attracted to them by a secret sense of the parallels between their situation and his. Lamenting a world occupied by "Cock-Sure Women" and "Hen-Sure Men," Lawrence complained in "Figs" that "the year of our women has fallen over-ripe," for, demanding an equal place in the sun, "our women" have horrifyingly "bursten into self-assertion."[22] In articulating such anxieties, however, Lawrence was really speaking for his generation of literary men both in England and America. Male novelists from James to Joyce were dismayed, as Robert Adams observes, by the world's "ready acceptance of frank unashamed trash" and specifically by the way in which "lowbrows avidly devoured rhetorical romances by such as Elinor Glyn, Marie Corelli, Mrs. Henry Wood, Miss Rhoda Broughton, Mary Elizabeth Braddon, Maria Susanna Cummins and other weird sisters."[23]

Perhaps the best example of the high-brow male modernists'

disgust with the low-brow female scribbler is Joyce's parody of Maria Cummins' *The Lamplighter* in the "Nausicaa" chapter of *Ulysses*. Writing in what he calls a "namby pamby marmalady drawersy style," he satirizes Gerty MacDowell's girls' school language, which both revolts and titillates him, for even as he attacks this vulgarly genteel virgin's sentimentality, he gets to transcribe not only her voice but the vices of one of the foremost of Hawthorne's "damned mob of scribbling women."[24] More recently, as if to summarize and clarify the feelings that fuel such satire, Nathaniel West in *Miss Lonelyhearts* helps his newspaper reporters revenge themselves against their own nihilism by letting them savor stories about lady writers with three names: "Mary Roberts Wilcox, Ella Wheeler Catheter, Ford Mary Rinehard..."—"what they all needed was a good rape"—and West records the men's special pleasure in the beating of a "hard-boiled woman writer" in a bar frequented by mugs: "They got her into the back room to teach her a new word and put the boots to her. They didn't let her out for three days. On the last day they sold tickets to niggers."[25]

Besides being driven to such ferocious misogyny and racism by feelings of anxiety and competitiveness, however, a number of modernist male writers became as enraged by their economic dependence on women as they were troubled by women's usurpation of the marketplace. A striking characteristic of the twentieth century *avant garde*, after all, was its determinedly anti-commercial cast. Perhaps there has been no circle of writers since the 16th century who were more dependent on private patronage; and like such 16th-century figures as Sidney and Spenser, Yeats, Lawrence, Joyce and Eliot, among others, were subsidized by a series of wealthy women or publicized by a set of powerful women. Yeats, of course, was financially dependent on Lady Gregory; Lawrence was sponsored by Ottoline Morrell and Mabel Dodge Luhan; Joyce was generously helped not only by Lady Gregory but also by Harriet Weaver and Sylvia Beach; Eliot was aided by May Sinclair and Virginia Woolf. In addition, all these men were in some sense at the mercy of entrepreneurial female editors like Harriet Monroe, Jane Heap, Margaret Anderson, Dora Marsden, and (even) H.D. Finally, the careers of such writers were significantly furthered by female facilitators like Amy Lowell, Gertrude Stein, Natalie Barney, Peggy Guggenheim, and Bryher.

But perhaps the most daunting aspect of women's entrance into literary history was the fact that some female authors were neither scribblers nor facilitators; some, quite terrifyingly, were great artists. Like Bret Harte, who may well have been as disturbed by Charlotte Brontë's power as he was dismayed by her popularity, such men as Poe, Hawthorne, Emerson, and Higginson brooded on the charismatic creativity of Margaret Fuller while others, like Henry James and Leslie Stephen, were awed by the mysterious mastery of George Eliot, an artist who, confided James, "has a larger circumference than any woman I have ever seen."[26] From novels like *The Blithedale Romance*, in which Hawthorne both celebrates and castigates the potency of Margaret Fuller as Zenobia, to stories like Kipling's "The Janeites," in which a World War I regiment becomes dependent on a lifesaving code evolved from characters in Jane Austen's novels, moreover, these writers demonstrate their sense of diminishment by a surprisingly strong female literary tradition. So large does this tradition loom in male imaginations that by the end of the 19th century a significant number of poets and scholars actually began to redefine their ideas about a classical history that had heretofore excluded the accomplishments of women: in *The Authoress of the Odyssey*, Samuel Butler proposes that Homer may at least in one of his epics have been a pseudonym for a woman, while such diverse figures as T.W. Higginson, Swinburne, Aldington, Robert Graves, and William Carlos Williams meditate on and translate the works of Sappho about whom Graves, in *The White Goddess*, reports one scholar remarking that "that's the trouble; she was very very good."[27]

But if these writers felt about so ghostly a precursor as Sappho that she might have been "very [threateningly] good," they were even more troubled by the competition of female contemporaries who might also be "too good." A kind of scribbling sibling rivalry is almost established between pairs like James and Wharton, Yeats and Lady Gregory, Hemingway and Stein, Lawrence and Mansfield (or H.D.), Wells and Richardson (or West), Eliot and Woolf, Graves and Riding, Miller and Nin, and in almost every case the male half of the pair devises a variety of strategies for defusing his anxiety about the threat represented by his female counterpart. Such strategies included mythologizing women in poems to align them with dread prototypes, fictionalizing them in novels to dramatize their destructive influence, slandering them in essays and memoirs, prescribing alternative ways of being for them in many genres, and ignoring or evading their achievements in critical texts.

James, for instance, mythologizes Wharton as "the whirling one... The Angel of Destruction,"[28] while Yeats—though he does not speak directly on the subject of Lady Gregory—displaces anxiety about female contemporaries into more general mythic statements about the woman artist. It is the dancer Loie Fuller's "dragon of air," for instance, that he remembers when he predicts the second coming of Herodias's daughters, and we are reminded that even the actress Maud Gonne's beauty "like a tightened bow" is potentially ruinous when the poet asks, "Was there a second Troy for her to burn?"[29] As for fictionalized portraits, Lawrence's versions of the artist as a young woman frequently emphasize her sterility as they recount the "frictional white seething" of her aesthetic as well as her sexual desire.[30] In *Women in Love*, Lawrence (at least in part) fictionalizes Katherine Mansfield as Gudrun, whose "nerve-brain" irony, together with her miniaturized art, suggest that her murderous rejection of Gerald is an expression of the implacable female will that manifests itself when women burst "into self-assertion," while in *Kangaroo* he even more frankly transforms H.D. into one of those "poetesses" his hero "feared and wondered over."[31]

But if Lawrence derogates Mansfield and H.D. in anxious or angry fiction, writers like Williams and Hemingway record distinctly unpleasant memories of such literary women in autobiographies and memoirs. Williams, for instance, consistently portrays H.D.—a woman toward whom he had once, admittedly, had romantic feelings—as foolish and pretentious. Similarly, but even more fiercely, Hemingway castigates his onetime mentor, Gertrude Stein, throughout *A Moveable Feast*. More generally, he vilifies the voracious mouths and wombs of literary ladies in a poem called "The Lady Poets With Footnotes":

One lady poet was a nymphomaniac and wrote for Vanity Fair.[1]
One lady poet's husband was killed in the war.[2]
One lady poet wanted her lover, but was afraid of having a baby
When she finally got married, she found she couldn't have a baby.[3]
One lady poet slept with Bill Reedy got fatter and fatter and made half a
million dollars writing bum plays.[4]
One lady poet never had enough to eat.[5]
One lady poet was big and fat and no fool.[6]

We might note that behind the misogyny of this catalog lurk Edna
St. Vincent Millay, Alice Kilmer, Sara Teasdale, Zoe Atkins, Lola
Ridge, and Amy Lowell.[32]

In poems and essays, Yeats, Lawrence, and Graves surface the
imperatives that underlie such misogyny when they admonish
female contemporaries and descendants to relinquish "self-
assertion" and, as Yeats tells his daughter, "become a flourishing
hidden tree," since for women in particular "an intellectual hatred is
the worst/So let her think opinions are accursed."[33] "The great flow
of female consciousness is downward," insists Lawrence, so that
"the moment woman has got man's ideals and tricks drilled into her,
the moment she is competent in the manly world—there's an end of
it."[34] Similarly, in *The White Goddess* Graves claims "it is the imitation
of male poetry that causes the false ring in the work of almost all
women poets," declaring that "a woman who concerns herself with
poetry" should either be "a Silent Muse" or should "be the Muse in a
complete sense... and should write... with antique authority,"[35] an
authority which, by its very antiquity, seems to preclude the threat
of contemporary competition.

Yet another way of precluding such a threat, however, involves
the construction of a literary history that denies the reality of
women writers, a gesture that returns us to the act of
Blutbruderschaft with American male precursors that Lawrence
performed in *Studies*. But it also reminds us that the existence of a
self-valorizing female tradition may have had to be more generally
countered with critical ceremonies of male self-certification so that
the emergence of modern male literary theoretical discourse,
exemplified by canon-forming works like "Tradition and the
Individual Talent," *The ABC of Reading, Seven Types of Ambiguity,* and

The Well-Wrought Urn, could be seen as an attempt to construct "his" story of a literary history in which women play no part. It is possible, indeed, that even a seminal study like *The Great Tradition*, which seems to acknowledge the existence of a female literary past, places the texts of major figures like Austen and Eliot in a context that desexualizes and therefore defuses their power. Perhaps to men from Hawthorne to Wilde and Beerbohm to Joyce, Lawrence, and Eliot a literary landscape populated by women, whether they were scribblers, facilitators, or great artists, would have seemed like a No Man's Land, a wasted and wasting country that left them with "an acute sense of disgrace."

Perhaps, too, the acute sense of disgrace we associate with the alienation and anomie of such a wasteland arises from the fact that, as much as the industrial revolution and the fall of God, the rise of the female imagination was a central problem for the 20th-century male imagination. Because texts like *Women in Love* and *The Waste Land, Ulysses* and "The Second Coming" have been universalized and privileged as documents in a history of cultural crisis, the sexual anxieties they articulate have been seen mainly as metaphors of metaphysical *angst*. But though they do, of course, express such *angst*—God did, after all, disappear in the 19th century and the smoke of dark Satanic mills did shadow Europe—it is significant that modernist formulations of societal breakdown consistently employed imagery that was specifically sexual and, even more specifically, imagery of male impotence and female potency.

Can it be that the literary sterility described by writers like Beerbohm, Huxley, and Hardy translated itself, paradoxically enough, into fertile imagery of biological sterility, castration, and impotence in modernist delineations of such famous figures as Eliot's Fisher King, Hemingway's Jake Barnes, Faulkner's Benji, Joyce's Leopold Bloom, and Lawrence's Clifford Chatterley? Can it be that the voracity of Yeats's "daughters of Herodias," the haunting ferocity of Stephen Daedelus's mother, the triumphant endurance of Faulkner's Dilsey or the necrophiliac potency of his Emily Grierson, the sinister wisdom of Eliot's lady of situations or his Madame Sosostris, and the virulent victories of Hemingway's Lady Brett reflect a corollary anxiety about a world in which women have "bursten into self-assertion"? As Theodore Roszak has shown, our assessment of early 20th-century intellectual history has been skewed because critics and scholars, whether consciously or not, have massively repressed the centrality of "the woman question" in this period.[36] But Virginia Woolf herself, after all, observed in 1928 that "no age can ever have been as stridently sex-conscious as our own; those innumerable books by men about women...are a proof of it," and she went on to speculate that "the Suffrage campaign was no doubt to blame. It must have roused in men an extraordinary desire for self assertion" (103). Thus, as Roszak and Woolf together imply, when we foreground women's increasingly successful struggle for autonomy in the years from, say, 1880 to 1920, we find ourselves confronting an entirely different modernism, a modernism constructed not just against the grain of Victorian male precursors, not just in the shadow of a shattered God, but as an integral part of a complex response to female precursors and contemporaries. Indeed, if Roszak and Woolf are right, we might hypothesize that a misogynistic reaction-formation against the risk of literary women became not just a theme in modernist writing but a motive for modernism.

Even the establishment of a supposedly anti-establishment *avant garde* can be seen as part of this phenomenon, for the twin strategies of excavation and innovation deployed in experimental works like *The Cantos, The Waste Land* and *Ulysses* reconstitute the patriarchal hierarchies implicit in what T.S. Eliot called in "Tradition and the Individual Talent" "the mind of Europe." More specifically, the excavation of that mind's fragments functions to recover and reinscribe the noble fatherhood of precursors from Homer to Shakespeare, while the linguistic innovation associated with the *avant garde*—the use of puns, allusions, phrases in foreign languages, arcane and fractured forms—functions to occult language and limit access to meaning so that only an initiated, even priestly elite can participate in the community of high culture. To be sure, a few women like Gertrude Stein and Djuna Barnes did intermittently join in such a community, but by and large it remained (and may have been unconsciously designed as) a men's club, and therefore it is not surprising that on his first reading of *The Waste Land* Joyce noted that T.S. Eliot's masterpiece "ends [the] idea of poetry for ladies."[37]

But how did the ladies react to such reactions? Did Woolf and her literary sisters form a women's club comparable to the male society created by Eliot and his brothers? Even more important, what did it mean for late 19th- and early 20th-century women writers that they no longer needed to "look everywhere," as Elizabeth Barrett Browning did, "for grandmothers, and find none."[38] These are issues which we have begun to explore in another paper.[39] Briefly, however, our research so far suggests that women experienced the dynamics of maternal literary inheritance differently from what we might expect if we only listened to the male side of the modernist sexual dialogue. Given the anxiety expressed by figures like Beerbohm, Huxley, and (to a lesser extent) Hardy, we might suppose that they were hearing fiercely exultant female voices, voices of "immense vitality" and victory. Strangely, though, when we turn to works by female contemporaries of, say, Beerbohm, we often find that such women feel imperiled rather than empowered by what has been defined for them as "the crime" of female literary ambition. Often, too, these women experience and express an "acute sense of disgrace" at least as intense as, though very different from, Beerbohm's, and they no doubt feel such shame precisely because texts like Beerbohm's tell them to. For, as is so frequently the case in the history of sex relations, men perceive the smallest female steps toward autonomy as threatening strides that will strip them of all authority, while women respond to such anxious reaction-formations with a nervous sense of guilt and a paradoxical sense of marginalization. At the same time, however, some women do feel empowered by every advance toward cultural centrality so we suspect we shall see, as we continue to study the particular issue of male-female literary relations in the modern period, that the female half of the dialogue is considerably more complicated than the male.

Interestingly, a poem Emily Dickinson wrote some years before the issue was so dramatically confronted by artists like Woolf and Eliot seems almost to predict the modernists' dilemma. Beginning in what appears to be the voice of the Ivy Wife, Dickinson articulates exactly the female exultation that men from Hardy to Huxley dread:

> I rose—because He sank—
> I thought it would be opposite—
> But when his power dropped—
> My Soul grew straight.[40]

Yet as she recounts the decline of her "fainting Prince," Dickinson's speaker becomes oddly anxious, even guilty, and in a desperate attempt to revive male power, she struggles to reconstruct her lover's history, telling him of "worlds I knew—/Where Emperors grew—." Finally, the fallen man becomes a burden that she has to strain to resurrect:

> And so with Thews of Hymns—
> And sinew from within—
> And ways I knew not that I knew—till then—
> I lifted Him—

Taken as a narrative, Dickinson's poem implies that the deconstruction of male primacy is not necessarily matched by a construction of female potency. Rather, male dis-ease is often balanced by female unease; for both sexes, the shock of the new—and specifically the new world of women's words—required shocking sociocultural redefinitions. T.S. Eliot himself may not have understood the radical implications of the relationship between tradition and the individual talent that he described in a 1919 issue of *The Egoist* (a journal, incidentally, which began its career as a suffrage periodical called *The Freewoman* and then *The New Freewoman*). But Eliot's theory that new works of art alter not only our sense of the past but also our sense of what art might *be* actually seems to articulate the sexual crisis that underlies modernism. For inevitably, the "ideal order" of patriarchal literary history was radically "modified by the introduction of the new (the really new) work of art"—and, as Woolf remarked, that "really new work" was women's work.

Notes

This essay was researched and written with the support of the Rockefeller and Guggenheim Foundations, both of whom we wish to thank. In addition, we would like to thank Ruth Stone, Elliot Gilbert, Cara Chell, and Stephen Wolfe for helpful advice and suggestions. Finally, we are grateful to colleagues and audiences at a number of institutions where we have tested out these ideas, including Georgetown University, Northeastern University, the California Institute of Technology, Southwest Texas State University, the University of Texas at Austin, the University of Delaware, and the School for Criticism and Theory at Northwestern University.

Epigraphs: Virginia Woolf, *A Room of One's Own* (New York: Harcourt, 1928), p. 68 (further citations will be included in the text); Gertrude Stein, *Everybody's Autobiography* (New York: Vintage, 1973; 1st pub. 1937); T.S. Eliot, "Tradition and the Individual Talent," in *Selected Essays of T.S. Eliot* (New York: Harcourt, 1950; 1st pub. 1919).

1. Unpublished letter, University of Sussex Library; we are grateful to the University of Sussex for allowing us to reprint this passage.

2. "The Crime," in Max Beerbohm, *And Even Now* (London: Heinemann, 1920), p. 246; subsequent page references will be included in the text.

3. Virginia Woolf, "Response to 'Affable Hawk' [Desmond MacCarthy]," in *The New Statesman*, 2 October 1920; reprinted in Virginia Woolf, *Women and Writing*, ed. Michele Barrett (New York: Harcourt, 1979), pp. 55-56.

4. See Ann Douglas, *The Feminization of American Culture* (New York: Knopf, 1977), *passim*.

5. Matthew Arnold, "The Scholar Gypsy"; James, *The Bostonians*, ed. Alfred Habegger (Indianapolis: Bobbs-Merrill, 1976; 1st pub. 1886), p. 318.

6. Harold Bloom, *A Map of Misreading* (New York: Oxford, 1975), p. 33.

7. Aldous Huxley, *Limbo* (New York: Doran, 1920), p. 2; further citations will be included in the text. In "The Manx Cat Again," forthcoming in the *Virginia Woolf Miscellany,* Joanna Lipking also offers an illuminating discussion of this Huxley tale.

8. All the James stories cited here are included in Henry James, *Stories of Writers and Artists*, ed. F.O. Matthiessen (New York: New Directions, n.d.); page references will be included in the text.

9. Thomas Hardy, "The Ivy Wife," in *The Complete Poems of Thomas Hardy*, ed. James Gibson (New York: Macmillan, 1976), p. 57.

10. Thomas Hardy, *Life's Little Ironies* (London: Macmillan, 1953; 1st pub. 1894; in a prefatory note, Hardy explains that "An Imaginative Woman" originally appeared in *Wessex Tales* [1888] "but was brought into this volume as being more nearly its place, turning as it does upon a trick of Nature, so to speak…."), p. 9; further citations will be included in the text.

11. Nathaniel Hawthorne's comment is quoted by Caroline Ticknor in *Hawthorne and His Publishers* (Boston: Houghton Mifflin, 1913), p. 142.

12. Quoted in Alfred Habegger, *Gender, Fantasy and Realism in American Literature* (New York: Columbia Univ. Press, 1982), p. 239.

13. Quoted in Cheryl Walker, *The Nightingale's Burden: Women Poets and American Culture Before 1900* (Bloomington: Indiana Univ. Press, 1982), p. 201.

14. Walker, p. 201.

15. See Nina Baym, *Woman's Fiction: A Guide to Novels by and about Women in America, 1820-1870* (Ithaca: Cornell Univ. Press, 1978), and Henry Nash Smith, "The Scribbling Woman and the Cosmic Success Story," *Critical Inquiry*, 1 (1974), 47-70.

16. Cited by Larzer Ziff, in *The American 1890s: Life and Times of a Lost Generation* (New York: Viking, 1966), p. 275.

17. Thomas Beer, *The Mauve Decade* (New York: Vintage, 1960), pp. 31-32.

18. For Stedman, see Walker, p. 117.

19. *The Artist as Critic: Critical Writings of Oscar Wilde*, ed. Richard Ellman (Chicago: Univ. of Chicago Press, 1982), p. 105; further citations will be included in the text.

20. See Bret Harte, "Miss Mix by Ch - l - tte Br - ntë," in *American Literature, Tradition and Innovation, II. Romantic and Realistic Writing*, ed. Harrison T. Meserole, Walter Sutton, and Brom Weber (Lexington, Mass.: D.C. Heath and Co., 1969; text taken from Harte, *Condensed Novels and Other Papers* [New York, 1867]).

21. Samuel L. Clemens (Mark Twain), *Adventures of Huckleberry Finn*, ed. James K. Bowen and Richard Vanderbeets (Glenview, Ill.: Scott, Foresman, 1970; 1st pub. 1885), pp. 120-21; further citations will be included in the text.

22. *The Complete Poems of D.H. Lawrence*, ed. Vivian de Sola Pinto and Warren Roberts (New York: Viking, 1964), p. 284.

23. Robert Martin Adams, *After Joyce: Studies in Fiction After Ulysses* (New York: Oxford Univ. Press, 1977), p. 5.

24. On Joyce's use of Maria Cummins's *The Lamplighter* (1854), see Anthony Burgess, *Joysprick: An Introduction to the Language of James Joyce* (New York: Harcourt, 1973), p. 103.

25. Nathaniel West, *Miss Lonelyhearts and the Day of the Locust* (New York: New Directions, 1962), pp. 13-14.

26. Henry James, letter to his father, 10 May (1869), quoted in Gordon S. Haight, *George Eliot: A Biography* (London: Oxford Univ. Press, 1968), p. 417.

27. Robert Graves, *The White Goddess: A historical grammar of poetic myth* (New York: Creative Age, 1948), p. 372.

28. For James on Wharton, see Cynthia Griffin Wolff, *A Feast of Words: The Triumph of Edith Wharton* (New York: Oxford, 1977), pp. 144-45.

29. William Butler Yeats, *Collected Poems* (New York: Macmillan, 1955), p. 89.

30. See, for instance, D.H. Lawrence, *Women in Love* (New York: Viking, 1960; 1st pub. 1920), pp. 454-55.

31. D.H. Lawrence, *Kangaroo* (New York: Viking, 1960; 1st pub. 1923), p. 253.

32. Ernest Hemingway, "The Lady Poets With Foot Notes," in *88 Poems*, ed. Nicholas Georgiannis (New York: Harcourt, 1979), p. 77.

33. Yeats, *op. cit.*, p. 187.

34. D.H. Lawrence, *Psychoanalysis and the Unconscious and Fantasia of the Unconscious* (New York: Viking, 1960; 1st pub. 1921, 1922), pp. 215-16.

35. Graves, *op. cit.*, p. 372.

36. Theodore Roszak, "The Hard and the Soft," in Betty Roszak and Theodore Roszak, ed., *Masculine/Feminine: Readings in Sexual Mythology and the Liberation of Women* (New York: Harper, 1969), p. 88.

37. Quoted in Richard Ellmann, *James Joyce* (New York: Oxford, 1959), p. 510.

38. *The Letters of Elizabeth Barrett Browning*, ed. Frederick G. Kenyon (New York: Macmillan, 1897, 2 vols. in one), I, 231-32.

39. See our "'Forward Into the Past': The History of Herland," unpublished paper delivered at California Institute of Technology, April, 1984.

40. #616, *The Collected Poems of Emily Dickinson*, ed. Thomas Johnson (Boston: Little Brown, 1955), pp. 303-04.

Bonnie Costello | *Response*

My response simply complements the excellent argument set forth in the paper you have just heard. Gilbert and Gubar focus on overt (if ironically presented) expressions of hostility toward women writers in fiction of the early modern period. Such expressions, they argue, constitute a reaction formation to the new dominance of the woman writer and to the emergence of female precursors. I want to suggest that as the avant-garde emerged to provide a new source of strength and collective identity for male writers in opposition to a feminized tradition, this hostility converted to a suspicious sort of praise. Precursors were named in order to be denied. Such praise undermined women writers by isolating them in conventional gender categories that diminish their power. (Gender identification from a feminist point of view may do equal damage, at times.)

Since Gertrude Stein was identified as the maternal lap of the Lost Generation, of course her foster sons had to abandon her in order to grow up. But that detachment is expressed not only in harsh invective such as Gilbert and Gubar find in Hemingway, but in such fond memory as Sherwood Anderson's.

> In the great kitchen of my fanciful world in which I see Miss Stein standing, there is a most sweet and gracious aroma. Along the walls are many shining pots and pans, and there are innumerable jars of fruits, jellies, and preserves. Something is going on in the great room, for Miss Stein is a worker in words with the same loving touch in her strong fingers that was characteristic of the women of the kitchens of the brick houses in the town of my boyhood. She is an American woman of the old sort, one who cares for the handmade goodies and who scorns the factory-made foods, and in her own great kitchen she is making something with her materials, something sweet to the tongue and

fragrant to the nostrils.[1]

Edmund Wilson quotes this passage in *Axel's Castle* as an example of Stein's importance to younger writers, so perhaps he shares in Anderson's ambivalence toward a female precursor. Marianne Moore gets cast in William Carlos Williams' autobiography as lovely, asexual Wendy holding together the Lost Boys in a literary Never Never land. Hers is a supportive role, "like a rafter holding up the superstructure of our uncompleted building."[2] Is Pound, in offering himself as the apologist of H.D.'s poetics really her sponsor, or is she made into the Pygmalion of his concepts when he advertises her as "H.D., Imagiste"? Modernism's power was associated with theory and while Joyce called manifestoes "mamafestas," few by women were printed.

Modernist men also warded off anxiety by acknowledging female power but renewing the division of labor. Women are repeatedly grouped together in criticism of the period as if, as in tennis or basketball, they couldn't hope to compete on the same court with men. Pound writes on Marianne Moore and Mina Loy, though a more likely comparison would be between Loy and Williams, or, God forbid, Pound himself. T.S. Eliot compares Moore to Christina Rossetti of all people: "And there is one final, and 'magnificent' compliment: Miss Moore's poetry is as 'feminine' as Christina Rossetti's, one never forgets that it is written by a woman; but with both one never thinks of this as anything but a positive virtue."[3] Eliot, the great arbiter of the literary tradition, defers from passing judgment about whether this poetry will last or not. Perhaps the most interesting, but more complex reaction to female power comes from John Crowe Ransom in his essay "Woman as Poet" from *The World's Body*. He offers higher praise of Marianne Moore than of others because her work has less "deficiency of masculinity" by which he means intellect. Edna Saint Vincent Millay is, for him, the characteristically strong female writer, so well endowed with the qualities of natural feeling.

The publicity so readily offered by male writers to their female colleagues often detracted from the work in drawing attention to the personality. Insofar as the "female writer" became worthy of notice, the writing itself got neglected. Moore was known for her braids and later her tricorner hat, Stein for her shape, her dress, and her lesbian eccentricities. "It always did bother me that the American public were more interested in me than in my work," she wrote. In the figure of Susan B. Anthony, Stein in "Mother of Us All" expresses her most personal irony; it is the story of a woman who won the public's attention, but not its understanding.

But for all this we should be wary of creating a no-win situation for male critics of the period, in which any remark is construed as disguised hostility, and no remark as designed indifference. There was much fair evaluation, negative and positive, of women by men. Discriminations should be made between the work of Sara Teasdale and the work of Marianne Moore. On the positive side it should be noted that Williams and Stevens remain two of the best critics of Moore. Stevens' essay "A Poet that Matters" offers an unambivalent celebration of Moore's aesthetic view of life. If writing by women was really a threat would Williams have made Moore the aesthetic hero of *Spring and All*, or have written such a bold defense of Gertrude Stein when others (male and female) disparaged her work? He not only acknowledged but advertised his female precursors. Eliot similarly used his influence to promote Djuna Barnes, and Randall Jarrell used his to promote Elizabeth Bishop. Such essays did not destroy but reinforced the public power of women writers. This fact does not, of course, contradict our speakers' thesis, but it suggests that caution is warranted. The Freudian reaction-formation theory is dangerously non-falsifiable.

Perhaps the real paradox our speakers point to is that male writers perpetuated negative myths while acknowledging positive realities about women writers. How could Williams celebrate Moore, then lapse into the Eliotic characterization of Marcia Nardi? The reaction-formation thesis is useful here. It might also be observed, though, that when women writers are seen as strong they are usually dissociated from sexuality (as opposed to gender). "Woman writer" was conceivable but never "wife/writer." Perhaps this is why H.D. has fared so poorly.

Finally, I think, the response of women to male anxiety is the more interesting and varied story and I look forward to our speakers' telling of it. The freedom from a patriarchal past, the redemption of language for modern experience, the possibilities of artistic community, the validation of eccentricity, all of these characteristics of the avant-garde attracted women writers. But they found that the new had a great deal of the old insofar as women were concerned.

Notes

1. Edmund Wilson, *Axel's Castle* (New York: Scribner's, 1931), p. 253.

2. *The Autobiography of William Carlos Williams* (New York: Random House, 1948), p. 148.

3. T.S. Eliot, rev. of *Poems* and *Marriage* by Marianne Moore, *Dial* LXXV (December 1923), rept. in *Marianne Moore: A Collection of Critical Essays*, ed. Charles Tomlinson (Englewood Cliffs, NJ: Prentice-Hall, 1969), p. 51.

Jeffrey Mehlman | Deconstruction,
Literature,
History:
The Case of
L'Arrêt de mort

In the already considerable annals of the naturalization of recent
French thought in this country, one of the most rewarding
documents is a collective volume of 1979 entitled *Deconstruction and
Criticism*.[1] Its publisher, Seabury Press, billeted the book a
"manifesto" of what has elsewhere been called the "Yale School":
Mssrs. Bloom, deMan, Derrida, Hartman, and Miller telling it as it
presumably never quite manages to *be*. The anthology, moreover,
was originally conceived as a series of readings of Shelley's dense
and elusive final fragment, "The Triumph of Life." There was, I
suspect, a measure of perfidy in that choice: the English poet falls
into a "trance of wondrous thought" and enters into dialogue with
his great French precursor, Rousseau.[2] For Bloom, Rousseau plays
Virgil to Shelley's Dante.[3] And therein lay the trap; for Shelley
ultimately supersedes Rousseau.[4] Consider that scenario as the
intertext of the anthology-manifesto: the "working through" of
Derrida, exemplary reader of Rousseau, in English would take the
form of allowing him to take his stand midst the enigmatic rhymes
of Shelley's most problematic poem—smack in the land of Bloom. If

there were ever terms on which the Frenchman (like Rousseau) might be superseded in and by English, these were they. The binding of the book, as if in anticipation, identifies the author as "Bloom *et al.*"

Derrida, in his shrewdness, was not about to fall into that trap, and his tack in retreating from—treating—Shelley's text lay in audaciously assuming as his own Rousseau's presumably imperfect English: "The Triumph of Life"? What if one were to hear "triumph" as the French verbal form: *(ce qui) triomphe de la vie*? As though the triumph *of* life might be appropriately (mis)read in French as a triumph *over* life. It is sufficient to assimilate that triumph over life to a death sentence—an *arrêt de mort*, as Blanchot entitled his short novel of 1948—for Derrida to land in familiarly uncanny territory. For it is indeed a reading of Blanchot's *L'Arrêt de mort* which is the core of Derrida's contribution to the "manifesto," the substance of what is in many respects a protracted epistle to the Americans.[5] It is that impressive reading which I propose to examine in these pages, with particular attention to its failure to deal with what I hope to show to be one of the novel's more disturbing intricacies: its way of negotiating its own perverse embeddedness in literary history and, ultimately, in European history *tout court*.

Let me begin by summarizing, however inadequately, the elusive events of *L'Arrêt de mort*. The book, something of a metaphysical ghost story, is divided into two sections. In the first, a narrator recalls a shattering experience he underwent in October 1938, during the most sombre days of the Munich crisis. Writing for him has since then been no more than the register of his retreat from its truth. An initial effort to give literary form to the events, in 1940, ended in the narrator's destruction of the manuscript. Indeed the work begins with a request never to disclose the "proof" of the events, to destroy without reading whatever pertinent documents the narrator may leave behind after his death.

Whereupon we are told of his ordeal, in those October days, when he is told by their common doctor that his friend J., an ailing young woman, has but three weeks to live. It is as though the death of the *other* brings home to the narrator the alterity of what, in

Blanchot's terms, can never be one's "own" death.[6] Part I then recounts the specific rhythm of his participation—or implication—in her agony—or "death sentence." He has a cast taken of J.'s hands; a palm reader consults the imprint of her *"ligne de chance"* and concludes: "She will not die." Particularly disabling pain-killers are administered. She asks to die: "If you don't kill me, you are a murderer." There hovers an almost Heideggerian wish to force death into a situation of "greater loyalty." Before she dies, he visits and has the impression of calling her back from death; she has an interlude of gaiety. Toward the very end, she pronounces the words *"une rose par excellence."* He believes she is referring to the flowers he has brought, and which, because of their strong fragrance, are kept outside the room. He is told that on the contrary, those were the "last words" she pronounced the previous night upon momentarily emerging from a coma. "This story chilled me. I told myself that the last night (*la nuit dernière*), from which I had been excluded, was beginning all over again (*recommençait*), and that J., drawn by some terrifying but perhaps also alluring and tempting thing, was reverting (*était en train de retourner d'elle-même*) to those last minutes when the long wait for me had been too much for her" (p. 44).[7] This "end" which "rebegins" in a moment of "return" provokes the precipitous end of Part I. J. wakes to point to the narrator and to say to the nurse: "Maintenant voyez donc la mort" (p. 48). He eventually seizes a large syringe and injects into her a quadruple dose of pain-killer. She dies.

The second part of the book relates more tentatively the narrator's subsequent liaison with a second woman, Nathalie. She is a translator of Russian and English, and the narrator knows the exhilirating irresponsibility of speaking to her in a foreign language. Indeed, gratuitously, he twice proposes marriage to her in her tongue. Now as the narrative develops, the reader and the narrator are overwhelmed by an odd aura of resonance between Nathalie and J. Could they, at some level, be the same woman? Is the narrator an unwitting Orpheus bringing back Eurydice from the dead? The climax comes when he discovers that Nathalie has taken his key and the address of the sculptor who had set the cast of J.'s hands. He insists that she renounce her "project." As if to remind us that whatever relation to Heidegger is being entertained in the text, it is not Sartre's, she responds: "It is no longer a project" (p. 123). Then: "You always knew?" Response: "Yes, I knew." Exaltation, triumph, jubilation at seeing "face to face what is alive for all eternity" (p. 125). By this time, moreover, the temporal—or historical—reference has become unhinged. The first pages of the book situate events on specific days in October, 1938, against the backdrop of the Munich accords. By the end of the book we are told that the dates may not be trustworthy, "for all may have transpired at a much earlier period." An eternal return erupts in 1938.

Let us turn now to Derrida's lengthy discussion of *L'Arrêt de mort*. It might well be extrapolated from his consideration of Blanchot's title; for the death sentence—an *arrêt de mort*—may also be read as a suspension or stopping (*arrêt*) of death.[8] Here then is a superb instance of a would-be "event" precipitated by its own deferment, and it may be imagined how that intuition might be developed into a reading of Blanchot's text as an exercise in deconstruction: an inconceivable *arrêt* which arrests itself, finding its locus in the interruption—or fold—dividing two apparently heterogenous *récits*.

What is initially most surprising in Derrida's essay is the conclusion: the "mad hypothesis" that "the two women should love one another, should meet, should be united in accordance with the *hymen*."[9] Hymen, the archaic French term for "marriage," is thus displaced from its initial mention in Derrida's text, where it refers to the narrator's gratuitous proposal of marriage to Nathalie, and becomes an imagined marriage, excluding the male narrator, between the two women who, in Blanchot's book, have no contact with each other, emerge from apparently separate narratives. But readers of Derrida will recognize the term *hymen* as an importation from his extended analysis of Mallarmé, "La Double séance."[10] In that text, *hymen*—like *arrêt* in the essay we are examining—is the pivotally perverse instance: at once consummation (marriage) and barrier preventing consummation (membrane). Let us precipitate matters and posit what is never explicit in the essay on Blanchot: Derrida's speculative conclusion, the presumably unspeakable revelation from which *L'Arrêt de mort* seems in retreat, would appear to assign as paradigm of Blanchot's text Mallarmé's masterpiece,

"L'Après-midi d'un faune." The male, in search of "trop d'hymen," dreams at high noon of interrupting the Lesbian embrace of two nymphs whose very dissolution into wakefulness is his own discomfiture.[11] The "mad hypothesis" consecrates a lineage that moves decorously from Mallarmé to Blanchot to Derrida. There is an interesting political point registered by that virtuality. In an excursus on J.'s vision (or mention) of "la rose par excellence," Derrida quotes Bataille's fragments on the death of his wife Laure, which transpired at exactly the time of J.'s death, October 1938. Her last words: "La rose."[12] We have, by implication, a gruesome version of Freud's paradigmatic *Witz*: two male friends (Blanchot, Bataille) share the pleasure of observing a woman compelled to leave the premises. Derrida's implicit critique is to imagine a man excluded, condemned, by the *liaison* of two women. For those who remember the day when the last word in avant-garde feminism consisted in quoting Derrida's line on wanting to write like a woman, the next (masochistic) step is indicated: I would like to write like, say, Charles Swann...[13]

Let us remain with the rose. Late in his volume of criticism, *L'Entretien infini*, Blanchot incorporated a short text, entitled in English, "A rose is a rose." It begins with an exorbitant formulation of the notion that the very will to develop one's thought is politically nefarious: "A thought that is elaborated, rendered rational, I would add, is a political thought, for the generality to which it tends is that of the universal State..."[14] Better, he suggests, the refusal to advance, the repetitive skid exemplified by Gertrude Stein's famous tag: "A rose is a rose..." Whereupon the author forgets Gertrude Stein and takes up the putative pretext of his essay: the "enigma of repetition" in a novel by Nathalie Sarraute.[15] Consider then that whereas *l'Arrêt de mort* gave us a political danger averted (Munich), a woman (J.) disappearing in the enigmatic repetition of the word "rose" only to be superseded by a second woman named Nathalie, the essay from *l'Entretien infini* repeats in the void that configuration, offers us its very ghost. As for the political peril, the "universal State," turn to the next essay after "A rose is a rose." It is called "Ars nova" and would also exonerate modernist art from a burden of political guilt. Its subject is Mann's *Doktor Faustus*, which, we read, erroneously metaphorizes twelve-tone music in its daring as an image of German history in this century: a pact with the Hitlerian demon.[16] Blanchot would free contemporary art from any contamination by that pact. From "A rose is a rose" to "Ars nova": "a rose is a *rosa*." But the pact with Hitler brings us back to Munich, the political catastrophe simultaneous with the first section of *l'Arrêt de mort*.

Might there then be a political legacy of Blanchot's rose? Consider the articulation of the pivotal episode in *l'Arrêt de mort*. It is while saying *rose* that "the last night" "rebegins," that J. enters her slide out of history into a death-like repetition. The narrator's initial thought is that she is referring to the flowers he has brought, and which she has given signs of wanting out of the room. But no, that reference—or situation—proves irrelevant, since the utterance "une rose par excellence" repeats her words of the "last night." Consider now that Blanchot's first separately bound publication on literature, "Comment la littérature est-elle possible?," is a commentary of 1942 on *Les Fleurs de Tarbes ou la terreur dans les lettres*.[17] The central conceit of Paulhan's essay is that poetry has traditionally—and unduly—exercised a reign of terror against *flowers* of rhetoric insofar as they are imagined as debased manifestations of linguistic repetition. In this, poetry has resembled that sign in the public park of Tarbes denying access to its garden to anyone who would enter its precincts with flowers in hand.[18] The room in which J. dies, that is, resembles Paulhan's garden in Tarbes: flowers had best be left outside. Blanchot, in his early essay on Paulhan, attempts to demonstrate, however, that iterability does not threaten poetic language from without, but is, on the contrary, a structure which contaminates poetry in its core: repetition is indeed the enabling condition of poetry. The Terror castigated by Paulhan—the search for the discursive equivalent of "virginal contact" with reality, what deconstruction would later thematize as "logocentrism"—is thus vitiated in its inception: "It is a matter of revealing to the writer that he gives birth to art only through a vain and blind struggle against it, that the work he believes he has reclaimed (*arraché*) from ordinary or vulgar language exists due to the vulgarization of virginal language, through an additional dose of impurity and debasement...he writes only through the help of what he detests."[19] But in precisely that manner was the narrator at J.'s deathbed chilled ("*glacé*") to realize that the repetition of a rose transpires outside and against the scenario of "Terror," without *reference* to those flowers he was advised to deposit outside J.'s room.

J.'s death in October 1938 or the untenability of (logocentric) terror, of Terror as logocentrism... In *Legacies: Of Anti-Semitism in France,* I have recently attempted to establish a connection between Blanchot's forgotten political writings of the 1930's, activist, fascist, a protracted apology for terrorism, on the one hand, and the metaphor of terror as an untenable discursive posture in "Comment la littérature est-elle possible?," on the other.[20] "Le terrorisme, méthode de salut publique" is a call for acts of terrorist violence against "the conglomerate of Soviet, Jewish and capitalist interests" governing France in 1936.[21] After the German reoccupation of the Rhineland in 1936, Blanchot's ire was above all directed at the "unfettered revolutionaries and Jews" who perfidiously "demanded against Hitler all possible sanctions immediately."[22] His text on the subject was entitled "Après le coup de force germanique" and appeared in April 1936.[23] It is anti-German, but above all French fascist. Two years later Munich would present a new "coup de force germanique." But by that time, I would submit, it was virtually impossible to maintain a line that was simultaneously "fascist" *and* "anti-German." For it should be underscored that those who did maintain a fascist line—Blanchot's position of 1936—in the wake of Munich tended massively to join the Collaboration a year or two later. Rebatet's comments on the situation in 1938, to cite the most notorious example, are virtually identical to those of Blanchot in 1936: "One of the vilest ignominies of the history of France will certainly have been the abominable blackmail to patriotism exercised by disarmers, wandering Jews, international socialists, etc."[24] But it is precisely at this point, October 1938, when one could no longer maintain a line that was both anti-German and pro-fascist (terrorist) that the scenario of the untenability of literary terror—or logocentrism—is (retrospectively) activated as the scene of J.'s death in *L'Arrêt de mort.*

Through a strange act of piety none of this political reality has entered the analysis of *L'Arrêt de mort*. That Blanchot's novel of Munich might be related to his exorbitant text on Jewish guilt in the wake of Hitler's "coup de force" barely two years before Munich does not enter Derrida's purview, for instance, in his ingenious text on that novel. A discussion of the multiple valences of Blanchot's "rose" is cut short by a self-addressed note in Derrida's running commentary: "Do not go on about the symbolism of the flower (have done so elsewhere, at length, precisely about the rose)."[25] The symbolism of the rose? The arresting of the play of Blanchot's signifier is simultaneous with an eclipse of the political reference. For "the rose," we are told, see *Glas*—rather than Blanchot on *Les Fleurs de Tarbes*. It is to that impoverishment of the intertextuality of Blanchot's *récit*, concomitant with an elision of all political reference, that I shall now turn.

There are several passing references in *L'Arrêt de mort* to J.'s mother, called ironically the "queen mother." Derrida is taken with the *insignificance* of the maternal point of origin, the mother as origin, in Blanchot's narrative, and rhapsodizes to that effect: "The figure of the mother, the 'queen mother,' a mere walk-on, almost a supernumerary, a figurant, a figureless figure, the vanishing origin of every figure, the bottomless, groundless background against which J.'s life fights, and from which it is snatched away, at every moment."[26] Now J.'s mother is indeed a walk-on, but it is important to realize from where she has arrived. There is an ironically conceived "queen mother" in Blanchot's *other* novel of 1948, *Le Très-Haut*.[27] She is the mother of the narrator and of his sister Louise. But Louise is as well the name of J.'s sister in *L'Arrêt de mort*. Derrida's "walk-on" mother has arrived, then, from *Le Très-Haut*. *Le Très-Haut*? The theological ramifications of Blanchot's novel have received their most extensive commentary in a Heideggerian context from Pierre Klossowski.[28] The Heideggerian reference, moreover, is all but dictated by the name of Blanchot's protagonist, *Sorge*, the key term for "solicitude" or "care" which irrupts midst a consideration of the *unheimlich* in the last chapter of the first part of *Being and Time*.[29] What I find most striking in Klossowski's reading is his failure to perceive that Blanchot's novel developed as a patent adaptation of the scenario of the Greek Orestes plays to a contemporary frame. It is sufficient to recount the plot to perceive this. Thus the anonymous author of the entry on *Le Très-Haut*, whom I have ascertained to be Michael Foucault, in Laffont-Bompiani's *Dictionnaire des oeuvres*: "Beneath a mask transposed from Greek tragedy—with a threatening and pitiful mother like Clytemnestra [our queen mother], a father who has disappeared, a sister caught-up in her savage mourning, an all-powerful and insidious step-father—Sorge is an Orestes become submissive, an Orestes solicitous of escaping from the Law in order the better to submit to it."[30] Blanchot's oft quoted line at the end of "La Folie du jour"—"Un récit? Non, pas de récit, plus jamais"—has led us not to expect the coherence of classical plot from his fiction.[31] In Derrida's terms, writing of *L'Arrêt de mort*: "In this sense, all organized narration is 'a matter for the police...'"[32] And yet the Electra-Orestes scenario, unnoticed by Klossowski, runs manifestly through *Le Très-Haut*.[33]

At this juncture, the question may be raised: if Louise "is" at some level Electra, who is her sister J. in *L'Arrêt de mort*? Classical tragedy provides but a single candidate, Iphigenia, condemned to death, and it is to a demonstration of Iphigenia's insistence as subtext of *L'Arrêt de mort* that I shall turn at present.

Note first that Euripides, our source here, composed, in accordance with the myth, two Iphigenia plays. In the first (in terms of plot sequence), *Iphigenia at Aulis*, the basis of Racine's play, Iphigenia is condemned to death so that Agamemnon's fleet might begin an unworthy war. In the second, *Iphigenia Among the Taurians* (Goethe's source), after the war, after committing his fatal deed of revenge against Clytemnestra, Orestes encounters in the land of the Taurians, modern Crimea, a foreign woman. She turns out to be Iphigenia herself, who, unknown to him, had been miraculously saved from sacrifice by the goddess Diana. In *L'Arrêt de mort*, then, as in the Iphigenia cycle, we find a bipartite structure, two separate units across which a woman, assumed to be dead, undergoes a miraculous and threatening return. Foucault, who perceptively detected Orestes in *Le Très-Haut*, sees no further than Orpheus, the organizing myth of *L'Espace littéraire*, in *L'Arrêt de mort*: Eurydice returning from the dead.[34] Let us see what he has missed in the process.

The setting of *Iphigenia At Aulis* is the Greek army mobilized but stalled in its wish to begin what is by common agreement a bad war. Helen of Troy is described as a "wicked wife," a "harlot."[35] Menelaus is told it is a blessing to be rid of her. The setting of the first part of *L'Arrêt de mort* is Munich: the French army is mobilized, but stalled, in what appears to have been a "dress rehearsal" for the beginning of World War II.[36] From the point of view of French fascism, it was a bad war, bound to end in disaster, and all for the sake of maintaining the "honor" of a despised regime, the Third Republic, disdainfully dubbed *la Gueuse*, the slut.[37]

At the beginning of the play, we find Agamemnon jealously guarding a secret—his intention to sacrifice his daughter, whom he has summoned on a false pretext of marriage—or rather trying to undo that secret, writing a letter to her attempting to defer "indefinitely" her arrival.[38] He is described by his puzzled servant as follows: "You have written upon this tablet which you carry about in your hands, then you scrape off your own writing. You seal your letter, then open it again, you throw it upon the ground..."[39] At the beginning of *L'Arrêt de mort*, we find the narrator jealously guarding a secret; instructions are given "above all not to open what is sealed...let [those who love me] destroy everything without knowing what they are destroying" (p. 10). Efforts to give form to the narrator's unrevealed obsession have led to an "unwriting" of his text which may be superimposed on Agamemnon's gesture: "In the lethargy (*desoeuvrement*) imposed by my stupor, I wrote this story. But once it was written I reread it and destroyed the manuscript..." In our two texts, then: secret, inscription, effacement.

Whereupon *l'arrêt de mort*, a death sentence undone, arrested, in its own execution. Euripides: "He [Agamemnon] will slash the poor girl's white neck with a sword."[40] Blanchot: "I took a large syringe, in it I mixed two doses of morphine and two of a sedative, four doses altogether of narcotics. The liquid was fairly slow in penetrating..." (p. 52). The injection precipitates J.'s death. For an uncanny responsibility is attributed to the narrator. J., just before the end, points to him and says to her nurse: "Look now and see death (*Maintenant voyez donc la mort*)" (p. 48). It is a revelation of the sort Euripides' Agamemnon manages to forestall until he is confronted with Clytemnestra's question: "Are you going to kill her?"[41] And then the infinitely imperfect "death" or "survival" of the victim. Blanchot's palm reader, consulting the cast of J.'s hands, had said: "Elle ne mourra pas." In Act III of Racine's adaptation of Euripides, Achilles says presciently: "Votre fille vivra..."⁴² Both are in their way correct. Significantly, in *Iphigenia at Aulis*, Euripides' final play, the confusion as to whether or not Iphigenia has died (or been replaced by a sacrificial deer) is simultaneous with a degeneration of the Greek text. The Hadas edition inserts the words: "From this point on, the Greek becomes more and more suspect."⁴³ The ending of the play as we have it is regarded as "spurious."⁴⁴ The play, that is, like Iphigenia, fails to *end*. And it is precisely that failure which Blanchot has given us as the death of J. in *L'Arrêt de mort*.

An interpretation? Earlier, in a discussion of the "rose" sequence of the novel, we superimposed the narrator's flowers, left outside J.'s room, on the *fleurs de Tarbes* which Paulhan's poet-terrorist would be forbidden to bring into the arena of poetry. J.'s repetition of "une rose par excellence" was taken to signify the ultimate untenability of (poetic) Terror, the irrelevance of the scenario of terrorism. But since Blanchot had been an ideologue or propagandist of terrorism a few years earlier, the dismantling of the terroristic—or logocentric—imperative was read as an encoded farewell to his investment in French fascism itself. The crux, it will be recalled, lay in the virtual impossibility in 1938 of retaining a line that would be simultaneously fascist and intent on resisting the peril for France represented by Germany. The painful solution: a farewell to the cherished eventuality of a fascist insurrection against the Republic, the dissipation of the hopes of 6 February 1934; the agonizing death sentence of J....⁴⁵ *Iphigénie '38* or *La Guerre de Troie aura lieu.*⁴⁶

Years pass. The war subsides. Orestes wanders in exile, bearing the burden of "the disasters of royalty."⁴⁷ He alights in the land of the Taurians, modern Crimea, charged with the mission of retrieving a sacred "image" of the goddess Diana. He encounters a redoubtable "stranger woman," whom he will recognize in a climactic scene as none other than his own sister Iphigenia, long believed to be dead.⁴⁸ Under Diana's protection, they flee the land of the Taurians together, intent on bringing the salvatory image back to Argos.

Now the second part of *L'Arrêt de mort*. The narrator, heir to the narrator of the first section, has slipped out of the historical past (Munich, 1938), and writes from a tentative present which has yet to transpire.[49] We are in the temporal medium initiated by the "rose par excellence," a last night about to rebegin. Within the ghostly exile of "literary space," the narrator wanders and encounters Nathalie. "Long afterward, she told me—and she remained convinced that I at no moment knew who she was, and that yet I treated her not as someone unknown, but as a person who was too well known" (p. 70). She is a foreigner, translating Russian and English, of manifestly "Slavic" appearance, perhaps from the region known as Crimea, the land of the ancient Taurians. Their exchanges find the narrator speaking her (foreign) tongue. There occurs, nevertheless, on the path to recognition, a crucial irruption of French: "It seems to me that something impelled me, a truth so violent that, breaking suddenly with the feeble bearings of that language, I began to speak in French, making use of insane words I had never before approached and which fell on her with all the power of their madness. No sooner did they touch her than I had the physical feeling that something had shattered. At that very instant, she was taken from me, ravished by the crowd, and the unfettered mood of that crowd, casting me at a distance, struck me, crushed me, as if my crime, become a crowd, was intent on separating us forever" (p. 103). The brute intensity of that contact in French, the narrator's mother tongue, is cut short. The recognition will be consummated, however, around the motif of a cast of her hands and head that Nathalie orders from the same artisan used by the narrator of the first part to retain an "impression" of J: "N'est-ce pas: vous l'avez toujours su?—Oui, dis-je, je le savais" (p. 124). In Goethe's *Iphigenia* (*auf Taurus*), a confusion is maintained between the sacred statue of Apollo's sister, Diana, on the one hand, and Orestes' sister, Iphigenia, on the other. In Blanchot's, no sooner is a statue invoked than the rhetoric of the book takes an unexpected turn toward the sacred: "And that at present that thing is there, that you have unveiled it and having seen it, you have seen face to face what is alive for eternity, for yours and for mine" (p. 125). With this conjunction of the statue and the sacred, however enigmatic their relation, it is as though the repertory of motifs from the second Iphigenia were complete: exile (or foreign tongue), recognition of the woman, statue, divinity, and triumph ("a glory which... touched me, myself, as well with the same grandiose pride, the same delirium of victory," p. 125).

But what are we to make of Blanchot's second installment? If *Iphigenia at Aulis* had been an encoded farewell to a no longer tenable fantasy of *action française*, indeed of fascism in France, what could be the parallel import of *Iphigénie among the Taurians*? In 1948, the year of *L'Arrêt de mort*, Blanchot published as well "La Folie du jour." Concerning that text, Emmanuel Lévinas, Blanchot's privileged reader, has suggested enigmatically that it was to find its proper application twenty years later in 1968.[50] During the failed political upheaval of that year, many were surprised to find Blanchot, participating in the *comité d'action écrivains-étudiants*, among the most politically active of French intellectuals.[51] Here, for example, is the text of a tract he composed in May of that year:

> In May, there is no book on May: not out of lack of time or necessity to "act," but through a more decisive obstacle: which is written elsewhere, in a world without presses, disseminated in the face of the police and, in a sense, with their aid, violence against violence. This suspension of the book (*arrêt du livre*), which is also a suspension of history (*arrêt de l'histoire*) and which far from bringing us to a stage prior to culture designates a point far beyond it is what provokes more than anything else authority, power, the law. May this bulletin perpetuate that suspension (*arrêt*), while preventing it from being suspended (*tout en l'empêchant de s'arrêter*). No more books, never again a book (*Plus de livre, plus jamais de livre*) for as long as we remain in relation with the turbulence of the break.[52]

The final lines ("plus jamais de livre") echo the end of "La Folie du jour" ("pas de récit. Plus jamais..."). But the play on *arrêt* and *s'arrêter* recalls specifically the verbal knot around which Derrida, for example, has built his reading of *L'Arrêt de mort*.[53] In 1936, Blanchot was calling for a renewal of the fascist insurrection against the Republic of February 1934. The ultimate failure of its eventuality, indeed of any authentic *action française*, I have suggested, was encoded in *L'Arrêt de mort* as the sacrifice of Iphigenia. In that context, I would suggest that the abortive events of May 1968—

arrêt qui s'arrête—find their prescient anticipation in the recognition of Iphigenia in the land of the Taurians: the moment in which the narrator draws on unimagined resources in French only to find Nathalie swept away by the crowd.[54]

That construct—Blanchot's politics of 1968 scripted by his rewriting of Euripides in 1948—finds unexpected confirmation in the writings of one of France's premier historians. In his recent memoir, Philippe Ariès, whose youth was passed in the ranks of *Action française*, recalls his astonishment at listening to the radio in May 1968: "What a surprise we had! Beneath the deluge of speeches and graffiti, we rediscovered the familiar themes of our childhood, of our reactionary youth: distrust of the centralizing State, an investment in authentic freedoms (*libertés réelles*) and in limited intermediary communities, in regions and their languages…. *Alors quoi?* What of it? What we, in the past, had loved, we, our parents and our grandparents, had been swept from our social milieu, from our political family, like so many fallen leaves, and here we saw them resurface at the other extreme (*aux antipodes*), midst young people who could be our children, to the left of a communism gone conservative…. There was indeed reason for astonishment. The shock was immense…."[55] Blanchot's affiliation before the war, *Combat*, was not classically reactionary, but represented something of a fascist (or national-socialist) dissidence within the Maurrassian context.[56] With that single modification, however, the reading of *L'Arrêt de mort* proposed in these pages would offer nothing so much as the scenario of the chiasmus informing Ariès' shock. Blanchot, propagandist in 1936 for a renewal of the rightist insurrection of February 1934, emerges from his literary labors, his explicitation of literature as the realm of "a passivity beyond all passivity," in order to join the leftist insurrection of May 1968. Midway between the two, he rewrites the Iphigenia cycle as part history, part anticipation of the entire sequence. In the first section, he dreams his implication in 1938 in the shattering (or apparent) death of Iphigenia or J. (I. or J.), figure of his generation's aspiration toward a no longer tenable fascism in France. In the second section—whose anticipatory status is uncannily conveyed in an opening paragraph: "all has not yet transpired"—Blanchot dreams a shocking recognition of the allegedly dead Iphigenia in the figure of the Slavic Nathalie. The political dream of insurrection is reemergent, but at the other end of the political spectrum: Iphigenia—or February 1934—will return as—the ultimate impossibility of—May 1968. After years in the desert of *l'espace littéraire*, the former partisan of *Action française* knows in his narrator a gust of French that transfixes him until Nathalie is swept away by the crowd. There will remain with him but the "truth" ("Vous l'avez toujours su") or "imprint" (*moulage*) of that chiasmus.

*   *   *   *   *

Ten years ago, in an analysis of Blanchot's writings on Rilke, I attempted to show that Blanchot's investment in the myth of Orpheus constituted a last metaphysical attachment to notions of archetype and originary voice which the very Rilkean corpus he was examining could be mobilized to dismantle.[57] Within Rilke's Orphic voice, I suggested, could be found a bizarre writing machine utterly disruptive of every mythic—and vocal—plenitude: Derrida, in brief, as the horizon of Blanchot's text.[58] In the years since then, Derrida has written his way into Blanchot's *oeuvre*, in a perspective ultimately compatible with that of my essay on Blanchot, Rilke, Derrida.[59] This was perhaps clear from my references to his analysis of *L'Arrêt de mort*: "L'Après-midi d'un faune" as implied subtext of Blanchot's *récit*; Mallarmé, Blanchot, Derrida as the pertinent line in French thought.

In these pages, I have departed from my program of ten years ago. Beyond the myth of Orpheus, quite properly detected by Foucault in *L'Arrêt de mort*, I have insisted not on a "writing machine" (Rilke's "phonograph" or Derrida's problematic), but on a second myth, Iphigenia, and the historical burden that it bears. If that reading has been able to convince, to impart something of the shock experienced by Ariès in the fragment of his memoir quoted above, I confess that I will shoulder any accusation of residual logocentrism or metaphysical deviation with relative calm.

Notes

1. H. Bloom, P. deMan, J. Derrida, G. Hartman, J.H. Miller, *Deconstruction and Criticism* (New York: Seabury Press, 1979).

2. "The Triumph of Life" in *The Selected Poetry and Prose of Shelley*, ed. H. Bloom (New York: Meridian, 1966), p. 363.

3. Ibid., "Introduction," p. x.

4. P. deMan, in his remarkable analysis of Shelley's poem (*Deconstruction and Criticism*, p. 42), summarizes—before challenging—the standard interpretation of the Shelley-Rousseau encounter: "Rousseau lacked power, but because he can consciously articulate the causes of his weakness in words, the energy is preserved and recovered in the following generation."

5. J. Derrida, "Living On," trans. J. Hulbert in *Deconstruction and Criticism*, pp. 75-176. The essay is accompanied by a running journal at the foot of its pages, studded with notes for the translator into English.

6. For Blanchot's comments on the "impersonality" or anonymity of death, see *L'Espace littéraire* (Paris: Gallimard, 1955), p. 204: "inevitable, but inaccessible death; the abyss of the present, a presentless time with which I have no relation, toward which I can not lunge, for within it, *I* do not die, I am stripped of the power of dying; within it, *on meurt*, there is dying, and the dying that never stops or ends."

7. Page references in the text refer to *L'Arrêt de mort* (Paris: Gallimard, 1948).

8. This observation, as Derrida acknowledges, was originally made by G. Hartman in his introduction to Lydia Davis' translation of *L'Arrêt de mort* in *The Georgia Review*, 30(1976), 379.

9. Derrida, "Living On," pp. 170, 172.

10. Derrida, "La double séance" in *La Dissémination* (Paris: Seuil, 1972), pp. 200-317.

11. The narrator, in Derrida's reading, might well end up with the Faun's lament:
    Mon crime, c'est d'avoir, gai de vaincre ces peurs
    Traîtresses, divisé la touffe échevelée
    De baisers que les dieux gardaient si bien mêlée.

12. "Living On," pp. 161-164.

13. In a recent text, culminating in a consideration of the sexual politics implicit in the writings of Lévinas ("En ce moment même dans cet

ouvrage me voici" in *Textes pour Emmanuel Lévinas* Paris: J.-M. Place, 1980), Derrida writes at times "as a woman" ("je parle depuis ma place de femme," p. 56). The essay regularly refers to Lévinas as E.L., thus toying with the French transliteration of the Hebrew designation for God, only to suggest in conclusion that E.L. might be appropriately misspelled as "Elle." Given the motif of the "Song of Songs" (and its dark Shulamite beauty) to which Derrida makes recurrent allusion, the entire development appears to move toward the punchline of the familiar joke from early in the astronaut era: "I have seen God and She is black."

14. *L'Entretien infini* (Paris: Gallimard, 1969), p. 498.

15. Ibid., p. 504.

16. Ibid., p. 507.

17. "Comment la littérature est-elle possible?" (Paris: José Corti, 1942).

18. J. Paulhan, *Les Fleurs de Tarbes ou la Terreur dans les lettres* (Paris: Gallimard, 1941), p. 26.

19. "Comment la littérature est-elle possible?," p. 24.

20. "Blanchot at *Combat*: Of Literature and Terror" in *Legacies: Of Anti-Semitism in France* (Minneapolis: University of Minnesota Press, 1983), pp. 6-22. Concerning the specificity of the (much abused) term "fascist" in this context, see also Z. Sternhell, *Ni droite ni gauche* (Paris: Seuil, 1983), p. 241: "Maurice Blanchot, in fact, furnishes the perfect definition of the fascist spirit by showing that what is at stake is a synthesis between a left abandoning its traditional beliefs, not in order to subscribe to the theses of capitalism but to define the true conditions of a struggle against it, and a right shedding the traditional forms of nationalism, not in order to subscribe to any internationalism, but rather to combat internationalism in all its forms." Sternhell, a political scientist, refers to Blanchot's "On demande des dissidents," *Combat* II, 20 (December 1937).

21. "Le terrorisme, méthode de salut publique" in *Combat* I, 7 (July 1936): "It is good, it is beautiful that these people—who believe they have all power, who make use as they wish of justice and laws, who appear to be the veritable masters of the beautiful blood of France (*du beau sang français*)—suddenly experience their weaknesses and that they be called by fear back to reason."

22. "Après le coup de force germanique" in *Combat* I, 4 (April 1936).

23. Ibid.: "Nothing could be as perfidious as that propaganda for national honor, executed by foreigners suspected by the offices of the

Quai d'Orsay, to precipitate young Frenchmen, in the name of Moscow or Israel, into an immediate conflict...."

24. L. Rebatet, *Les Mémoires d'un fasciste, I: Les Décombres* (Paris: Pauvert, 1976), p. 108. Rebatet offers an impressive account of the paralysis of the right at the time of Munich under the heading: "Au sein de l'Inaction française," pp. 115-137.

25. "Living On," p. 155.

26. Ibid., p. 131.

27. *Le Très-Haut* (Paris: Gallimard, 1948), p. 59: "I recalled that Louise referred to her only as 'the queen.'"

28. P. Klossowski, "Sur Maurice Blanchot" in *Un si funeste désir* (Paris: Gallimard, 1963), p. 171: "Henri Sorge? Should we not read that name in the language of the Holy Empire of Metaphysics and translate: Heinrich Sorge? Or rather: *die Sorge* as understood at the University of Freiburg? A *cura, cura pura*? a pure *souci*—camouflaged under the name of Henri. A pure *souci*, such is existence: the *Dasein* of Henri...."

29. M. Heidegger, *Being and Time*, trans. J. Macquarrie and E. Robinson (New York: Harper & Row, 1962), pp. 225-273.

30. Laffont-Bompiani, *Dictionnaire des Oeuvres* (Paris: Laffont, 1957), VI, 512. The same paragraph appears in M. Foucault, "La pensée du dehors," *Critique*, 229 (June 1966), pp. 536-537. For the Orestes-Sorge connection, see, in particular, the visit to the tomb in *Le Très-Haut* (Paris: Gallimard, 1948), pp. 73-74: "And now I have sworn: there where an unjust death occurred, there shall be a just one...."

31. "La Folie du jour" (Paris: Fata Morgana, 1973), p. 33.

32. "Living On," p. 105.

33. In his eloquent discussion of *Sorge* in *Martin Heidegger* (New York: Viking, 1978), p. 100, G. Steiner comments that Sartre's Orestes, in *Les Mouches*, was plainly imagined within the medium of Heidegger's thoughts on the "uncanny" (*unheimlich*) and "homelessness" (*das Nichtzuhause-sein*). Blanchot's Orestes, Sorge, is then something of a corrective to Sartre's reading of Heidegger. Blanchot's reservations about *Les Mouches* appear in "Le Mythe d'Oreste" in *Faux pas* (Paris: Gallimard, 1943), pp. 72-78. For a remarkable (anti-Sartrean) reading of *Les Mouches*, see D. Hollier, "I've Done My Act: An Exercise in Gravity" in *Representations* 4 (1983), 88-100.

34. Foucault, "La Pensée du dehors," p. 539: "There are narratives, like *L'Arrêt de mort*, consecrated to the gaze of Orpheus...."

Rilke's text of 1919 about a primitive phonograph ("Ur-Geräusch") and the *Sonnets to Orpheus.*

59. See, in addition to "Living On," Derrida's, "Pas" in *Gramma* 3/4 (1976), and "La Loi du genre" in *Glyph,* 7 (1980).

Naomi Schor | *Response*

Piety, I would submit somewhat provocatively, may well be the key word in Jeffrey Mehlman's remarkable reading of Blanchot's *L'Arrêt de mort.* The word piety occurs in a crucial transitional passage in Mehlman's text when he is attempting to account for Derrida's seemingly unaccountable "elision of all political reference" in his reading of Blanchot's work. Mehlman writes: "Through a strange act of piety none of this political reality has entered the analysis of *L'Arrêt de mort.* That Blanchot's novel of Munich might be related to his exhorbitant text on Jewish guilt in the wake of Hitler's "coup de force" barely two years before Munich does not enter Derrida's purview, for instance, in his ingenious text on that novel." What then, as Derrida might ask, is piety? The OED provides the following definition: "1. an early form of pity; 2. habitual reverence and obedience to God, devotion to religious duties and observances, godliness, devoutness, righteousness; 3. faithfulness to the duties naturally owed to parents and relatives, superiors, etc; dutifulness, affectionate loyalty and respect especially to parents." According to Mehlman then, Derrida's failure to bring into play Blanchot's terroristic journalism of the thirties is imputable to some singular form of love and respect for a spiritual father. Now I would like to suggest that the strange act of piety here is not Derrida's, rather

Mehlman's own. For by ascribing Derrida's failure to what is after all a loving gesture, Mehlman designates his own gesture of veiling what may be a far more serious reason for Derrida's omission.

In order to elucidate the scenario I have sketched let me begin at the beginning, that is with Mehlman's title. But immediately a problem presents itself: which title? the title which appears on the printed program for this lecture series or the title of the paper actually presented, for you will have observed that they are not the same. The superimposition of the first title, "Literature versus History" on the second, "Deconstruction, Literature, History" raises precisely those questions which Mehlman's psychoanalytic interpretation of Derrida's omission obscures, namely: what is the relationship between these terms: is it adversary (emphasis on the *versus* in literature versus history) or rather merely disjunctive (emphasis on the asyndetic structure of the second title). Our superimposition yields one striking piece of evidence: the introduction of the third term, deconstruction, effects a breakdown of the rigid traditional opposition between History (Truth) and Literature (Fiction). What then, the question arises, is the relationship between the reading practice we have come to know as deconstruction and history? According to Jonathan Culler in his recent book *On Deconstruction:* "Deconstruction's dealings with history...remain for many an obscure point."[1] For others the point is not so much obscure as it is sore: "Is deconstruction merely," the author of another of the current guides to deconstruction asks, "as some of its opponents claim—a newfangled textual mystification, helping to keep history and politics at bay?"[2] The question of the relationship of deconstruction and history is not one admitting of simple answers and I can only refer those who wish to pursue the question further to Derrida's major pronouncement on the subject, which appears in one of the interviews reprinted in *Positions.* There, in answer to a question posed by two members of the then Marxist *Tel Quel* regarding his conception of history, Derrida answers that he is skeptical of the *"metaphysical* concept of history" (i.e. history as linearity, teleology, etc.), yet retains the word "history" in order to, in his own words, "produce another concept of history or conceptual chain of history,"[3] that is, one that would take into account the play of *différance*. Now whatever the place of history by deconstruction, both deconstruction's champions and its detractors agree that as a reading practice it has never relied on or appealed to History as a ground for meaning. Therefore there is nothing strange or pious about Derrida's a-historical reading of *L'Arrêt de mort*. But, of course, Mehlman's concern is with the erasure of *political* and not *historical* references in Derrida's reading. The slippage from history to politics is regrettable, for Derrida's suspicion of history (in the conventional sense) and historicism does not in any way signify a retreat from politics. Thus while labeling Derrida's writings "grossly unhistorical," Terry Eagleton writes with evident approbation: "Derrida is clearly out to do more than develop new techniques of reading: deconstruction is for him an ultimately *political* practice."[4] Indeed, Derrida's reading of *L'Arrêt de mort* is eminently political if the field of politics includes in its purview textual, sexual, and institutional politics.

What I am arguing then is that by suggesting that Derrida's reading of *L'Arrêt de mort* is aberrant, rather than consonant with a deliberate and general reading practice and, further, a-political rather than properly speaking a-historical, Mehlman is performing his own strange act of piety, refusing to confront the very real possibility that for purely theoretical reasons the difficult articulation he is attempting between deconstruction, history, and literature may be doomed to failure and that he may in some sense have to renounce deconstruction. And yet, on another level, the level of interpretation, that is exactly what he does. By rejecting Derrida's Sapphic—which is to say feminist—reading of the novel in favor of Foucault's Orphic reading, Mehlman is choosing between what Edward Said described in his now classical article on Derrida and Foucault, as "two exemplary positions": Derridean textuality and Foucauldian worldiness.[5] Given the history of poststructuralism, the playing off of Foucault against Derrida cannot, as we say in our terroristic vocabulary, be innocent.

But, of course, Mehlman is not content to stay with Foucault's mythic reading of *L'Arrêt de mort*; instead, in a brilliant re-reading of Blanchot's infinitely re-interpretable text, he proposes *Iphigenia* as privileged subtext. Now as brilliant as this reading is—and I confess

I found it quite dazzling—I remain unpersuaded by its ultimate conclusion, which is to say its *telos*. I am referring to Mehlman's suggestion that the "abortive events of May 1968—*arrêt qui s'arrête*— find their prescient anticipation* in the recognition of Iphigenia in the land of the Taurians." In other words, 1968 would represent the return in chiasmatic form of the terrorist ideology Blanchot espoused and promoted in his youth.

Now even or perhaps especially to the non-historian that I am— and in many ways a historian would have been the ideal discussant for this interdisciplinary paper—such a reading must give pause, for it seems to legitimize a version of the events of 1968 at variance with most available accounts, which are more likely to stress the students' and workers' debt to the writings of Marx than to those of Charles Maurras. The covert continuity of Fascism and the worker-student uprising of May 1968 that Mehlman's reading of *L'Arrêt de mort* presupposes may or may not exist—the instability of the binary pair Left/Right pervades much current political thought in France— but if Mehlman wishes to persuade us of the truth of his controversial reading—a hypothesis every bit as "mad" as Derrida's—then adequate proof must be given. And that proof is simply not forthcoming. All that we are given is Philippe Ariès's "unexpected confirmation" of the author's "construct." It is at this critical juncture in Mehlman's text that the repressed or unaddressed theoretical question of the articulation of deconstruction, literature, and history returns, though in a somewhat different form. The question now becomes: is it possible to write or rewrite history without relinquishing some of deconstruction's more ludic modes of reading, modes of reading many of us, including myself, have practiced and which privilege serendipity and even synchronicity?

At the end of his paper Mehlman envisages the eventuality of future accusations of "residual logocentrism" with Olympian calm. It would indeed be easy enough to meet Mehlman's challenge by suggesting, for example, that Terrorism, when it is not Fascism, serves in his text as a sort of transcendental signifier grounding meaning. One could also argue perversely, as I have in a sense just done, that Mehlman is insufficiently logocentric. A potentially more productive approach beckons at this point: one that would eschew the undeconstructed paradigm deconstruction/logocentrism altogether. Finally, taking up again a word whose Kantian resonances Derrida has recently explored, I would suggest that what is needed today in our reading of texts, and especially those involving the grave issue of the part played by Fascism in modern French intellectual history, is less piety and more respect.

Notes

1. Jonathan Culler, *On Deconstruction: Theory and Criticism after Structuralism* (Ithaca: Cornell Univ. Press, 1982), p. 128.

2. Christopher Norris, *Deconstruction: Theory and Practice* (London: Methuen, 1982), p. 75.

3. Jacques Derrida, *Positions*, trans. Alan Bass (Chicago: University of Chicago Press, 1981), p. 56 and p. 57.

4. Terry Eagleton, *Literary Theory: An Introduction* (Minneapolis: University of Minnesota Press, 1983), p. 148.

5. Edward Said, "The Problem of Textuality: Two Exemplary Positions," *Critical Inquiry* 4 (1978), 673-714.

Lawrence Lipking | Night Thoughts on Literary History

I am going to tell you a story that you have never heard before. It seems strange to me that this story should be unknown, for it concerns perhaps the most famous and influential descriptive passage in Western poetry. Yet the story is of a kind that we do not tell very well today. It deals with what poets know about the world and what they learn from each other—in short, with what we used to call literary history. All literary history, we hear these days, consists of stories: narratives constructed about the past, stitching the documents together in a more or less pleasing pattern. But somehow those narratives have become less convincing in the last generation. It is as if our stories about literature, like our fairytales, relied on assumptions about the coherence of the past and the justice of the world that not even the best tellers of tales could credit any more. In some of the original versions of one favorite, the experts inform us, the wolf eats Red Riding Hood up and gets away with it. Those versions make as good sense as any other in our world. What could be more arbitrary, after all, than a happy ending? Hence the stories we tell each other about literary history have begun to take some peculiar twists. There is the wolf's version, for instance: the slaughter or gobbling of all his precursors, those fathers or haggard grandmothers, in order to clear some space for himself. There is the daughter's version: silenced by a patriarchy that has cut her throat before she could let out a cry. And the grandmother seems too pious and doddering for her version to make any sense. Nor does great poetry necessarily live happily ever after. So my story may not be convincing. Perhaps it may seem pedantic, or sketchy, or rather too neat. That may be the fate of any literary history today. But whether or not it has a persuasive point, my story will have a moral. I do not propose it as a model for all literary history but as a means of testing the storytelling project itself: its adequacy, its way of shaping the past to fit our own needs and interests, its twists and turns, the lies it tells, its future. My moral will be that not all tales are the same. Some stories work better than others.

This story begins, like most good stories, with Homer. At the end of Book Eight of *The Iliad*, the Trojan forces have driven the Greeks back to their ships when night descends. Hektor decrees that his troops will camp out, lighting fires to keep the enemy from escaping by darkness. The campfires are set, and then the poem brings forth a simile:

ως δ δτ εν ουρανωι αστρα φαεινην αμφι σεληνην
φαινετ αριπρεπεα οτε τ επλετο νηνεμος αιθηρ
εκ τ εφανεν πασαι σκοπιαι και πρωονες ακροι
και ναπαι ουρανοθεν δ αρ υπερραγη ασπετος αιθηρ,
παντα δε ειδεται αστρα, γεγηθε δε τε φρενα ποιμην

Here is Fitzgerald's translation:

As when in heaven
principal stars shine out around the moon
when the night sky is limpid, with no wind,
and all the lookout points, headlands, and mountain
clearings are distinctly seen, as though
pure space had broken through, downward from heaven,
and all the stars are out, and in his heart

the shepherd sings: just so from ships to river
shone before Ilion the Trojan fires.

This simile may be the most celebrated ever composed, and I want
to linger on it. But a preliminary question ought to precede analysis:
what is the simile *for*? That question has often puzzled critics of
Homer. The answer cannot be that the simile defines or elucidates
the original object of its attention; for in fact the image of a moonlit
night does not help to clarify the picture of the campfires. From
what angle of vision do such fires resemble the stars? What
equivalent of the moon can shine in the Trojan camp? (Is it Troy?
Does Hektor's watchfire so much dwarf the others?) Only two
points of comparison really seem relevant: the stars and fires are
bright and there are a great many of them. But the simile provides
much information that distracts us or leads us away from the
Trojan camp: the moon, the lookout points, the radiance of
heavenly air, the shepherd's heart. No mountain clearings huddle
on the plains of Troy. Evidently our questions about the *exactness* of
the comparison only tempt us to miss the point. But what then *is* the
point?

Scholars have offered many sorts of answers. Technically, we
might note that the narrative requires a pause here, after the shock
and swift motion of the battle scenes. The audience is given a
chance to relax and luxuriate in beauty, to make ready for night.
(The night that follows will be the longest in *The Iliad*, two books
long, with the embassy to Achilles and the raid on the Thracian
bivouac.) Moreover, the poet cleverly deepens the sense of night by
comparing one night-scene with another; from classical times this
passage has been called Homer's "nightpiece." But perhaps more
important, the simile is to be enjoyed in its own right. The Greeks
prized vividness of presentation, the sheer exercise of imagination,
and the process by which stars are superimposed on campfires
invites the listener to join in making a picture. That is what similes
are for. They cue us to notice that something is happening,
something that might be called poetry, by diverting us from action
to the activity of creation; they force us to cooperate in turning the
mixture of signs into significance, and reward us by the pleasure we

find in our work. However we solve the riddle—how are fires like stars?—the answer we arrive at will be the right one for us. The passage is particularly satisfying because this situation is worked into the simile itself. The classicist C.C. Felton, who thought this simile "the most magnificent that can be conceived," notes that the "inexpressibly beautiful" climax with the shepherd's rejoicing "heightens the effect of the visible scene, by associating it, in the most direct and poetical manner, with the inward emotion that such a scene must produce."[1] To put this another way: Homer introduces an observer in order to remind us of the delight in our own observing. Our hearts are cheered because the scene is *clear*—not all spelled out, but open to the view. Hence the shepherd is a surrogate for the listener, and what we take joy in, like him, is the perfect transparency of the scene: the act of creation in which we participate.

But the moonlight is not so clear. Ever since ancient times critics have worried the fact that the simile, brief as it is, commits two anomalies. Both of them may be spotted by any reader who is willing to do something very unfashionable in literary criticism these days: go out on a moonlit night, look up at the sky, and compare the poetry with what the eyes see. The first problem is what Leaf describes as "the obvious difficulty that stars are *not* visible 'about the bright moon.'"[2] The light of the moon drowns them out. One group of textual scholars has gone so far as to amend the Greek so that it means "*new* moon," a sliver that will not interfere with starlight. But a more ingenious interpretation is implied by Fitzgerald's use of the word "principal" (for the Greek *ariprepéa*, "very bright"), which suggests an optical illusion that any stargazer can test. When the moon is full, its brightness submerges all nearby stars of lesser magnitude. Yet to the naked eye the effect may seem quite different: *first*-magnitude stars or planets near the moon may look unusually bright, precisely because they no longer compete with the myriad sprinkles of light around them. The wash of moon that effaces the stellar small fry serves also to isolate the principal stars in a bowl of emptiness. I think that Fitzgerald is right, and that is what Homer meant us to picture. I think so because I have seen it with my own eyes.

The second anomaly is less easy to resolve. It concerns the line that in Fitzgerald's version may seem most striking of all: "as though/ pure space had broken through, downward from heaven." (Cf. Lattimore, "as endless bright air spills from the heavens.") The Alexandrian editors were nervous about this line, and they had reason to be, since the plain sense of the words suggests shafts of light breaking through clouds and up to now Homer has been describing a cloudless night. Some editors excise the line, which however ruins the poetry. Others have tried to justify the image logically, which in my view does not work. What accounts for such an obvious contradiction? The explanation in fact is easy. It lies in the nature of formulaic composition. Two of the lines of the "nightpiece" recur word for word in Book Sixteen of the *Iliad*, when Patroklos drives off the Trojans, "As when the lightning master,/ Zeus, removes a dense cloud from the peak/ of some great mountain, and the lookout points/and spurs and clearings are distinctly seen/ as though pure space had broken through from heaven...." The line fits perfectly there; and when the author of the *Iliad* hits upon an elegant and metrical formula, he is seldom content to use it only once. That leads to some problems, unfortunately, for careful readers, who object to the moon breaking through clouds that are not there (in the earlier passage). But Homer does not seem much concerned about such problems. Unsophisticated listeners will not notice them; sophisticated readers may actually relish the mysterious or uncanny effect by which moonlight suddenly intensifies on a clear night, as if the cloud it broke through were not in nature but in our perceptions.

Though critics may be disturbed by these anomalies, moreover, later poets have reason to be grateful for them. When Homer nods he wakes his followers up; they suddenly have something to do, a gap to fill or an error to correct. Many of the nightpieces in Western poetry might be regarded as efforts to set Homer straight. At the same time, since Nature and Homer are the same, poets take a fix on the moon by using the coordinates of the Greek. The history of poetry may be charted, according to Harold Bloom, by observing each poet's misreading of his percursors. But many poets read quite accurately. Comparing the text of nature with the nature of the text, they work out a better description, paying homage to Homer by noticing what he has gotten wrong or left out. Thus poetry keeps its momentum. The light that breaks so oddly through cloudless clouds in the *Iliad* has proved to be one of the most productive anomalies in literature. Poets still have not exhausted its potential.

My story skips a few millenia and lands on Alexander Pope. Pope knew quite well what was wrong with Homer's lines. But he also knew that his job was not to criticize but transmit them, turning them into elegant English verse to make them a shining example:

> As when the Moon, refulgent Lamp of Night!
> O'er Heav'ns clear Azure spreads her sacred Light,
> When not a Breath disturbs the deep Serene;
> And not a Cloud o'ercasts the solemn Scene;
> Around her Throne the vivid Planets roll,
> And Stars unnumber'd gild the glowing Pole,
> O'er the dark Trees a yellower Verdure shed,
> And tip with Silver ev'ry Mountain's Head;
> Then shine the Vales, the Rocks in Prospect rise,
> A flood of Glory bursts from all the Skies:
> The conscious Swains, rejoicing in the Sight,
> Eye the blue Vault, and bless the useful Light.

These lines are among the most admired and reviled in eighteenth-century poetry, and they need a careful inspection. But once again I want to ask my preliminary question: what is this passage *for*? The answer is not, I think, to remind the reader of campfires. Given these lines alone, only a Sherlock Holmes among readers would ever guess that they referred to the Trojan camp. Nor does the answer seem to be, as with Homer, that the reader has been stirred to pleasurable imaginative activity; for Pope's explicit and fluorescent painting does not leave much to the imagination.

A better answer, in my view, is that Pope is trying to persuade us that something is happening—the something, in this case, not being campfires or even poetry but Homer's nightpiece. That was the translator's problem. It would not be enough for him to render the sense of the Greek. Rather, what he needed to communicate was (in Pope's appropriate word) Homer's *fire*. The reader must stop and take notice; a great passage is going by. Such motives are not very popular with translators or readers today, but we should not dismiss them too lightly. An English version that allows us to skim the lines without pausing has not done the simile justice. Consider a translation that was intended specifically to correct Pope's excesses, the "plain and unelevated" words of another great poet, William Cowper:

As when around the clear bright moon, the stars
Shine in full spendor, and the winds are hush'd,
The groves, the mountain-tops, the headland-heights
Stand all apparent, not a vapor streaks
The boundless blue, but ether open'd wide
All glitters, and the shepherd's heart is cheer'd.

These lines are clean and accurate and economical and virtuous. All decent people should admire them. But not much seems to be going on in them. A few minutes after looking through this passage, most readers will have forgotten that it ever existed. And Pope was not willing to allow that to happen. Indeed, another answer to what his translation was for would be that he wanted his readers to memorize it and quote it whenever they looked up at a moonlit sky. That may seem a lot to ask, but there is one argument in its favor: thousands of English readers, during the next century, did exactly what Pope wanted. They knew the nightpiece by heart.

Not many readers do today. When Coleridge, in a crucial footnote to the *Biographia Literaria*, cited Pope's lines as a vicious example of "pseudo-poetic diction," he spoke for a change in taste that most later generations have taken for granted. To us Pope's art seems labored. He ornaments and embellishes the plain sense of the Greek until it has become twice as long and half as natural. Much of the problem, to be sure, may rest not with Pope but with how badly we read him. When Coleridge quotes the lines, from memory, he mangles the first image into "resplendent lamp of light," himself creating the absurdity he goes on to criticize. Pope chose his diction with care. "Refulgent," for instance, still kept its original meaning of "shining by reflection," a precise and witty description of the "lamp" of the moon, which does not shine by its own light; and "conscious," to take another example, is an exquisite modifier for the swains, who are not only internally aware of what they see but aware of "knowing together" (the original Latin sense). Most moderns, like Coleridge, do not read Pope with attention. Moreover, we tend to be deaf to his music. Leigh Hunt accused Pope's nightpiece of rhythmic monotony because of its unvarying accents (the caesura occurring always at the fourth or fifth syllable); but Steven Shankman has lately pointed out that the sound echoes the sense: "Pope is in this particular passage describing a hauntingly silent scene and the couplets should therefore be perfectly balanced and regular so as to convey as little nervously animated movement as possible."[3] In fact the rhythm is perfectly calculated as a slow and stately progression to the climax on "A Flood of Glory," followed by a decrescendo on the swains. If we do not hear such effects in the first place, we will not remember them later.

The essence of Pope's art in the nightpiece, however, is less musical than pictorial. It is a masterpiece of rococo design. One way of talking about this would emphasize the simultaneous limitation of scale and addition of intricacy. Pope converts the vast outdoors into a sort of interior, with its lamp and throne and pole, as if a painted stagedrop had replaced the infinite sky. The effect is of a solemn *scene,* where the comparison deals less with campfires and stars than with raw nature and her imitation in a theater or cathedral.[4] The lighting resembles stage lighting, a sequence in which each part of the set in turn is illuminated—or rather, gilded and tipped with silver. No threat of any outward untamed force disturbs the calm theatricality of the design. But a better way of describing the art of the passage, I believe, would stress its affinity with painting. A connoisseur of *ut pictura poesis,* Pope arranges the scene by touching in each of its details, complete with its color values: the yellow gilding on the dark trees, the silver tips of the mountains, the blue of the "vault." A painter would have no difficulty copying the nightpiece. Yet the meaning conveyed by this picture is subtle. To be specific: what Pope is imitating in this canvas is not only Homer but several famous paintings of the Adoration of the Shepherds (here pluralized from Homer's single swain). It is this imitation that accounts for the persistent religious overtones in the rhetoric—"sacred," "solemn," "glory," "bless," etc. Whether we experience this effect unconsciously or, like the shepherds, through a communal act of knowing, it conditions all our responses. The poet induces us to take part in a Catholic ceremony, adoring a glory from heaven. To be sure, there is no Christ-child in this painting. But that something is missing is exactly what persuades us that something is happening in Homer's passage. Just as the shepherds feel that some unknown event has changed their lives, so the reader feels a mysterious unseen presence behind the description. The nightpiece is sacred; it tells us to worship its revelation, even if we do not understand the language in which it appears to us. Hence, like Virgil in the Fourth Eclogue, Homer has created an expectation that only the Messiah could fill. Silent night, holy night, all is calm, all is bright—the new dispensation will tell us what words to add.

At the same time, Pope quietly adjusts the text to remove each of its anomalies. He had felt somewhat testy, a footnote shows, about the charge that Homer neglects the fact that "the Light of the Stars is diminished or lost in the greater Brightness of the Moon": "I see no Necessity why the Moon may not be said to be bright, tho' it is not in the full. A Poet is not obliged to speak with the Exactness of Philosophy, but with the Liberty of Poetry." Yet in his own version the problem disappears: "Around her Throne the vivid Planets roll,/ And Stars unnumber'd gild the glowing Pole." The vivid, first-magnitude planets shine near the moon, while ordinary stars are scattered indefinitely through the "Pole" or sky. When Coleridge commented that the Greek "(i.e. the stars around, or near the full moon, shine preeminently bright) conveys a just and happy image of a moonlight sky: while it is difficult to determine whether in [Pope's lines] the sense or the diction be the more absurd," he was inadvertently revealing his own carelessness about "the Exactness of Philosophy." Pope watched what he was doing. In the same way, the second anomaly is cleverly mended by the careful placement of "Then." The sequence is ambiguous in English. We are free to interpret the burst of light not as something that happens *after* the initial cloudless shining (as in the Greek) but as something simultaneous with it (*when* the moon shines, *then* shine the vales). The static, painterly arrangement of the English scene conceals the momentary confusion of the Greek, its lurch across time. Pope has corrected Homer. We may feel, of course, that something is lost by the change—not only the accidental mystery of the original but also its pace and its freshness. Pope knew what risk he was taking. "It is the most beautiful Nightpiece that can be found in Poetry"; and to improve such beauty by trueing it with science and Christianity might also be to kill it. Yet English poetry needed a perfect model: a Homer with no spot or flaw.

During the following century many readers turned to Pope for that model. As late as 1781, when Samuel Johnson published his "Life of Pope," the *Iliad* seemed a place for young poets to start. Johnson pays special attention to the nightpiece. He prints all the manuscript variants, the slow progress from "As when *in stillness of the silent night*" to final refulgence, and then adds this comment: "Of these specimens every man who has cultivated poetry, or who delights to trace the mind from the rudeness of its first conceptions to the elegance of its last, will naturally desire a greater number; but most other readers are already tired, and I am not writing only to poets and philosophers." Schoolteachers may have been more exacting. Those who wanted to make their pupils into poets and philosophers knew that the way lay through Pope. Thus Wordsworth tells us that he was forced to memorize hundreds of Pope's lines, surely including the nightpiece. There was a predictable outcome: he never forgave him.

Indeed, the importance of the revenge that Wordsworth and Coleridge took on this passage can hardly be exaggerated. In my opinion, Pope's version of the nightpiece is the single most important brief source of Romantic poetry. That will be the climax of my story. It ought to be surprising; for, so far as I can find, no previous scholar has even mentioned the lines as a source for Wordsworth. Nor is the reason for this omission hard to find: Wordsworth himself savaged the lines. His most direct assault occurs in his most defensive piece of criticism, the "Essay, Supplementary to the Preface" (1815). Between the time of *Paradise Lost* and *The Seasons*, he argues there, hardly a poet in England looked at nature:

To what a low state knowledge of the most obvious and important phenomena had sunk, is evident from the style in which [Pope has executed] his translation of the celebrated moon-light scene in the Iliad. A blind man, in the habit of attending accurately to descriptions casually dropped from the lips of those around him, might easily depict these appearances with more truth. [Pope's lines], though he had Homer to guide him, are throughout false and contradictory. The verses of Dryden, once highly celebrated, are forgotten; those of Pope still retain their hold upon public estimation—nay, there is not a passage of descriptive poetry, which at this day finds so many and such ardent admirers. Strange to think of an Enthusiast, as may have been the case with thousands, reciting those verses under the cope of a moon-light sky, without having his raptures in the least disturbed by a suspicion of their absurdity.

The force of this verdict is striking. It is not a part of my story to judge between Pope and Wordsworth, or to measure which one is more absurd, but clearly both Coleridge and Wordsworth find it singularly galling that people recite Pope with pleasure while attacking them for not being true to nature. Passion like this must have a cause. At least a part of that cause, I believe, is that Wordsworth was haunted by the nightpiece—perhaps, when young, had even recited it under a moon-light sky—and needed to prove what a distance he had come from it. Thus his first major poem, *An Evening Walk*, concludes with a nightpiece that may sound oddly familiar: "But now the clear-bright Moon her zenith gains,/ And rimy without speck extend the plains;/ The deepest dell the mountain's breast displays,/ Scarce hides a shadow from her searching rays...." Pope is by no means the only source of these lines (another source is the nightpiece in Thomson's *Seasons*— partially based on Pope). But the very idea that Wordsworth's poetry (even when derivative as this) might derive from other poetry rather than from observation makes him prickly and nervous. A long time later, he wrote this about *An Evening Walk*: "There is not an image in it which I have not observed; and now, in my seventy-third year, I recollect the time and place where most of them were noticed." One translation of this remark might be, "despite appearances Pope has nothing to do with the way I looked at the moon—I simply used my own eyes." But modern critics have learned to be suspicious of Wordsworth's eyes. He saw nature, as the rest of us do, as he had been trained to see it; and his insistence that the eye of the Poet be "steadily fixed upon his object," that the job of the Poet be to "faithfully and poetically describe the phenomena of nature," tends to beg the question of how every description modifies that object and those phenomena through the very process of putting them into words. Is Wordsworth himself "true" to nature? That must depend on what we mean by truth. For Wordsworth, one definition of truth in description was that it be unmediated by the arts of allusion and painting—in short, that it be the opposite of Pope.

Yet Pope came back to haunt him. One fine example is a poem of which Wordsworth was especially proud, and which many scholars consider one of his breakthrough works—a piece in which he found his real voice. When first written, in January 1798, it was labelled a "Fragment." But at its first publication, in the same volume where Pope's lines were denounced, it took on the title of "A Night-Piece".

———The sky is overcast
With a continuous cloud of texture close,
Heavy and wan, all whitened by the Moon,
Which through that veil is indistinctly seen,
A dull, contracted circle, yielding light
So feebly spread that not a shadow falls,
Chequering the ground, from rock, plant, tree, or tower.
At length a pleasant instantaneous gleam
Startles the pensive traveller as he treads
His lonesome path, with unobserving eye
Bent earthwards; he looks up—the clouds are split
Asunder,—and above his head he sees
The clear moon, and the glory of the heavens.
There, in a black blue vault she sails along,
Followed by multitudes of stars, that, small
And sharp, and bright, along the dark abyss
Drive as she drives;—how fast they wheel away,
Yet vanish not!—the wind is in the tree,
But they are silent;—still they roll along
Immeasurably distant;—and the vault,
Built round by those white clouds, enormous clouds,

Still deepens its unfathomable depth.
At length the Vision closes; and the mind,
Not undisturbed by the delight it feels,
Which slowly settles into peaceful calm,
Is left to muse upon the solemn scene.

I do not wish to build a case for the specific influence of Pope on these lines. Surely coincidence might explain the way that two poets, looking at the moon, perceive it surrounded by stars, in a "blue vault" where its light seems like "glory," and note "the solemn scene" alike. But I do think it unlikely that any contemporary reader, coming upon Wordsworth's poem after reading his essay, could help comparing the two nightpieces. The title itself issues a challenge.

Viewed as an answer to Pope, "A Night-Piece" clearly takes its stand with prolonged and specific attention to nature. The poet not only casts his gaze to the sky, he keeps it there. Moreover, he presents the whole scene as it appears to the eyes of a single observer—or rather, two successive observers, since the opening veil of clouds could not have been seen by the "unobserving eye" of the traveller. Wordsworth tries to see as fully and innocently as possible. One remarkable testimony to that innocence is the description of the rapid motion of the moon and stars as they sail and drive and roll—"how fast they wheel away." Obviously this motion is an illusion. It is the clouds, not the stars, that are moving and tricking the eye (as a landscape "moves" through a train window). Yet Wordsworth relies so heavily on reporting what he "sees" that he manages to forget how to interpret it, as if the traveller had been startled back into childhood or the first visions of Adam. Pope could not have written thus. When *he* describes an optical illusion, he always finds some way of letting us know that he knows it is an illusion. But Wordsworth remains within the focus he has chosen.

The main difference between "A Night-Piece" and its predecessors, however, is the moment on which it centers: not the moon in a cloudless sky but the moon as it breaks through the clouds. Homer's anomaly here takes over the poem, with its mystery not dispelled but somehow deepened. The natural process itself assumes the burden of that mystery, inspiring a vision at once normal and unfathomable. Overcast clouds do break, of course, even without the agency of Zeus, and the light of the sky suddenly falls on us in a different way, but the ordinariness of the phenomenon does not make it less strange. The effect is heightened by Wordsworth's second departure from earlier nightpieces, his subtle conversion of the delighted shepherd into a traveller whose reactions guide our emotions not only at the end of the passage but throughout it. This maneuver gains some advantage. Foremost, one might argue, is the way that the reader is gradually lured into the poem (as in Gray's *Elegy*) by a shifting perspective that begins with a neutral observer (or Dorothy Wordsworth, on whose journal entry the description is based), moves to a certain "pensive traveller" (who may or may not be the poet), and ends in a mind that belongs to the reader as much as to anyone else. We muse along with the poet. And a second advantage is that the passage is dynamic, not static like Pope's. It drives from one mood and one time to another, from the feeble light behind clouds to the light that breaks through, and creates an unsettling scene from the tension between them. This is no painting; it moves like the moon in the clouds.

There is also some disadvantage. The particularity of Wordsworth's lines, their ties to a specific series of moments and minds, also makes them peculiar. Such light is not "useful." It would do no good to memorize this passage, for one would never find a night appropriate for reciting it; nor could one compare it to campfires or anything but itself. For contemporary readers this lack of usefulness was fascinating. Perhaps it is even the essence of Wordsworth's poem. When Crabb Robinson was given these lines as a specimen of "imaginative power," he commented that "They are fine, but I believe I do not understand in what their excellence consists. Wordsworth, as Hazlitt has well observed, has a pride in deriving no aid from his subject." A harsher critic might have responded like the first readers of *Lyrical Ballads*, as Wordsworth imagined them: "They will look round for poetry, and will be induced to enquire by what species of courtesy these attempts can be permitted to assume that title." Not even Wordsworth himself immediately recognized that his nightpiece was a poem; seventeen years went by before he published it. Only when the "Fragment" turned into "A Night-Piece" did it claim the sort of power we associate with poetry, the implicit contract that promises the reader some experience that, if not exactly "useful," is worth musing about.

What is the source of that power? A host of modern critics have tried to account for it, and a number have written very eloquently about "A Night-Piece." Kenneth R. Johnston's fine essay "The Idiom of Vision" may be taken as representative. Beginning with a question that resembles those I have asked about Homer and Pope—"Does something happen in 'A Night-Piece' or not?"—it arrives at the conclusion that the poem itself, or at any rate the story of how it gropes toward understanding, is what happens: "The meaning of 'A Night-Piece,' like most of Wordsworth's descriptions of vision, resides in the process it describes: simultaneously disjunctive and conjunctive, the very type of a great consummation in which Mind and Nature are imagined as exquisitely fitted to each other, yet remain distinct."[5] Many Wordsworthians would agree with this answer, and I do not wish to quarrel with them. But a reading of "A Night-Piece" that places it in the context of literary history, not merely among Wordsworth's moments of vision (capped above all by his apotheosis of the nightpiece in the ascent of Snowden), might arrive at a different conclusion. First of all, we notice the conspicuous omission of the clues that lend the earlier descriptions their interest: Homer's comparison of stars with campfires and Pope's intimation of a sacred hidden presence. By contrast, Wordsworth seems to insist that we pay attention to the experience for its own sake. The poetry consists in this act of attention. Indeed, the passage might even be taken as an allegory of how to pay attention. The traveller is stirred not by any prior idea or will to significance but by an involuntary response. The vision is a *gift.* Perhaps his original numbness, "with unobserving eye/ Bent earthwards," is the necessary condition for the delight he later feels. Someone perpetually alert and alive to art, someone like Pope, could hardly be vulnerable enough to take in the full joy of "a pleasant instantaneous gleam." The glory of heaven breaks through best for those who are looking elsewhere. Poetry too depends on a wise passivity to set up its acts of attention. We give but what we receive.

"A Night-Piece" conveys another moral as well. For many contemporary readers, the surprise of the poem may have come not only from the absence of a story but from the satisfaction that the poet and traveller find in what they see. Many other nightpieces had been composed between Pope and Wordsworth, and few of them had aimed to calm their readers. Dark fantasies and night thoughts lurk in the standard eighteenth-century night. From the time of Young, a passage like the first seven lines of "A Night-Piece" had prepared an audience for terror and melancholy and violent death. Wordsworth reverses that trend. Nothing that he taught Coleridge was more important than the insight so beautifully conveyed in "The Nightingale" and "Frost at Midnight": to the person at home in nature, night is a scene of joy. One only has to know where to look. In this respect, Wordsworth's variation on the classical nightpieces of Pope and Homer—a moment of calm and cheer snatched from the violence that surrounds it—is not a repudiation but a fulfillment of their art. He returns to the spirit of the earlier poems and associates joy with the night. That is what the traveller and the reader have learned to do at the end of the passage: to have their expectations of darkness disturbed by delight, and to muse on a scene that, while solemn, contains no threat that attention cannot dispell. Wordsworth restores to the nightpiece its moment of quiet.

My story should not end here. Ideally a historian would follow the scene through many more transformations: its conversion, in the Snowden episode, to a type of universal mind; the gentle reference in Coleridge's "Limbo," where Homer himself may have inspired the "sweet" reciprocation of a blind man's face to the face of the moon; the nightpieces of Hugo and Shelley; or the absorption of the moon into pure language in Mallarmé. But many moons would be needed to perform such an exercise, and I have promised you a moral. What is the point of telling a story like this?

My first moral is so obvious that it would hardly bear mentioning, were it not that so many theorists now suspect that it has been refuted. I refer to the assumption that the history of poetry is continuous; that poets draw not only on each other but on phenomena that change little if at all over time; and that the historical search for the source or origin of a poem may also provide the key to understanding it. Homer may wax and wane, and the moon change its spots, but they still set the terms on which nightpieces come into being. We cannot read well without learning what stories apply. I do not mean to imply by this that poetry is always the same in every age or that only one story can be told about it. Many other narratives could be constructed around my sequence: for instance, the shift from oral to written poetry, or the movement from Homer's "star-system"—that is, a world in which a few heroes shine brighter than ordinary mortals—to Pope's hierarchical universe, in which God stands to rulers stands to people as Homer stands to translator stands to audience, to Wordsworth's levelling, in which no distinction is maintained among poet, traveller, and reader or between heaven and the mind. More simply, the thread of the story might be increasing selfconsciousness, or the shift from the naive to the sentimental, as Homer's love of a story yields to an interest in how the story is told. All these narratives, and others, seem plausible to me, and each of them can serve as an instrument for analysis. What does not seem plausible to me is the refusal of narrative. Ever since the time of the New Criticism, literary historians have been made to feel uneasy about going outside a poem in order to explain it; and the increasing specialization of literary history has also worked to inhibit the comparison of poems from different periods and languages. Not many Romantic scholars seem to know or care that anyone before Wordsworth had written a nightpiece.[6] This seems to me a mistake. We need to tell each other stories in order to remember that poetry is a living and changing thing.

We also need to keep our eyes on the moon. When Wordsworth suggested that his own poems had rejected cheap enchantments in order to deliver a faithful record of nature, when he announced his own preference for things over words, he was undoubtedly stretching a point. Modern critics have turned him back into words, and perhaps that is where a poet belongs. But the process may have gone too far. As I hope to have demonstrated, a brief study of the night sky yields dividends in perceiving what Homer and Pope were trying to do, and Wordsworth himself seems to have read them with half an eye on the moon. Descriptive poetry requires such attention; not because it offers a "faithful record" but because the tension between what the eye sees and what it wants to see, between verse and accuracy, the spirit and the letter, is exactly the source of its interest. Homer adjusts the campfires to the stars, Pope designs a painting while checking its details against Newton, and Wordsworth sacrifices his knowledge of astronomy to a gaze that knows nothing but what is directly before it. We appreciate such scenes partly by noticing what is not there. Thus all three nightpieces contain the same false note: a full-orbed moon that does not dim the stars. Ancient editors, we have seen, would like to have imposed a *new* moon on Homer. Pope fretted about the problem, but could not bring himself to reduce the size of the moon. And Wordsworth, whether or not he was aware of these precedents, followed them all too well. The only detail in Dorothy's journal entry that "A Night-Piece" omits is its final phrase, on the stars: "Their brightness seemed concentrated, (half-moon)." With her usual exactness, she knows the reason why the stars look bright: a half-moon. But Wordsworth's poem suppresses that information. He allows or encourages the reader to imagine a full moon instead. And the motive is not hard to guess: full moons *look* better in a nightpiece, grander, more shining. All poets know that, whatever they know about stars. Yet critics are free to hold a poem to the truth. And this conflict of motives leads to my second moral: one means of learning what poems do is to watch what their stories leave out.

Much of my story, in fact, records something missing. If the effect of Homer's simile depends partly on its incorporation of a different night into its scene, and if the missing Christ-child breathes hints of transcendence into Pope's sacred painting, then Wordsworth achieves his effect partly through obliterating Homer and Pope. An undercurrent of suspense runs through such passages. As in a murder mystery, they lead us on by dropping clues that we may or may not be able to make use of. Poets rely on such methods for persuading us that more may be happening than we can quite understand. And so do literary historians. Their stories invite us to add dimensions to poems, dimensions of time and context, until we begin to see what is there and what maybe is not. A well-known literary historian once told me that something I had written had "filled a much-needed gap." I am willing to take that as a compliment, for it defines a part of the work of every literary historian. We fill in the gaps that poets need to create, the gaps between poets or within them, and in so doing we provide an illusion of continuity in which the poet can pick a new hole of his own. The relation is symbiotic: we need to find something there so that an artist can still find something missing. Meanwhile the moon waits on, always ready to be misperceived in some ingenious new way.

But I do not want to emphasize only mistakes. There is also a more positive reading of my story, and that is the moral on which I should like to end. The stories told by literary historians are not so arbitrary as theorists have lately insisted. To be sure, we have many reasons to be uneasy. Much of the older history was built on assumptions that cannot stand up under careful scrutiny: the assumption that historical method could divorce itself completely from values or ideologies and arrive at a Mecca called "objectivity"; the progressive or teleological assumption that history works toward a single, well-defined goal (as if the road to Xanadu could not also be mapped as a detour to Limbo or Erewhon); the assumption that a work of art is the lump sum of its sources or the data of its author's life; the assumption that the meaning of a poem can be paraphrased and exhausted; the assumption that the existence of the moon can be considered independently of the ways we perceive and describe it. Not all of the older literary history is compromised by such assumptions; but theorists are not the only ones, these days, who scorn the claims of history to truth. The story can always be told in another way. Indeed, I am well aware that my own narrative about nightpieces, whether or not convincing in its own terms, might be considered merely the latest version of the old source studies, "explaining" each poem by tracing it back to some origin that retreats, like a will-o'-the-wisp, the more it is sought.

Am I not the very person I warned you against?

Perhaps I am; but here is my side of the story. Literary history is a shifty and awkward and devious kind of work, and perfection is not to be expected of it (any more than of literary theory). But sometimes it does advance a little toward better knowledge; its stories ring truer. I think we are gradually learning to tell them better. My story today may serve as a modest example. Obvious though it may seem, it has never been told before. But the credit for that does not belong to me. A generation ago, most of the elements of such a narrative could not have been used, for not even very learned critics would have known how to see them. The analysis of Homer as an oral poet who deals in formulaic units, the analysis of Pope as a master of literary pictorialism, the analysis of Wordsworth as a poet who achieves his effects by knowing what to leave out, has not been available to historians until recent times. We still have not absorbed the significance of such lessons. The literary histories that will replace the histories of past generations are only beginning to be written. But I think that their time is coming. Specifically, it seems possible that the next generation will witness a kind of literary history that does not yet exist: a history of poetic *style*. Such history will not be grounded, like older histories, on the notion that poetry can be classified according to its subject matter (as if the meaning of night were the same for all poets) or that there is only a single right way of reading. It will be attentive to small things, like changes in prosody, and to large, like such questions as what happens in poetry and what poetry is for. It will also ask questions we have not yet learned to ask. I do not pretend to know what those questions will be, let alone how to give all the answers. But my story today is intended as part of that story.

Notes

1. *The Iliad of Homer*, tr. William Cowper (New York: Appleton & Co., 1860), p. 203n.

2. *The Iliad*, ed. Walter Leaf (London: Macmillan, 1900), I, 369n.

3. *Pope's "Iliad": Homer in the Age of Passion* (Princeton, N.J.: Princeton Univ. Press, 1983), p. 145.

4. In his enormously popular *Meditations and Contemplations* (1748), James Hervey praises Pope's nightpiece as follows: "What a *majestic Scene* is here! Incomparably grand, and exquisitely fine!—The Moon, like an immense crystal Lamp, pendent in the magnificent Ceiling of the Heavens. The Stars, like so many Thousands of golden Tapers, fixed in their azure Sockets...."

5. "The Idiom of Vision," in *New Perspectives on Coleridge and Wordsworth*, ed. Geoffrey Hartman (New York: Columbia Univ. Press, 1972), p. 25.

6. An interesting exception is Neil Hertz' brilliant "Wordsworth and the Tears of Adam," in *Wordsworth*, ed. M.H. Abrams (Englewood Cliffs, N.J.: Prentice-Hall, 1972), which compares "A Night-Piece" to Milton but omits all poetry of the intervening century and a half.

Ruth Whitman | Response

I have always believed that useful literary criticism of whatever school—historical, teleological, structuralist, deconstructionist— has one essential purpose: to drive the reader back to the text.

Mr. Lipking's discussion of Pope's translations of Homer, the treatment of the two so-called anomalies in the "nightpiece" simile in Book VIII of the *Iliad*, and Wordsworth's reactive use of the passage in his own "Nightpiece" caused me—and perhaps it is the reaction of a poet—to want to see what Homer really said in the lines of the simile; how he said it and why he said it. It seems to me I cannot respond to anyone else's response to the passage until I have examined its language carefully. With the aid of the indispensable Liddell and Scott *Greek-English Lexicon*, I looked up the key words of the Homeric passage and retranslated it:

> As when in the sky the prominent stars show forth
> around the radiant moon, and the cloudless air
> is still, and all the lookouts and high headlands
> and valleys appear; then from the sky the light
> of heaven overflows, making vivid
> all the stars, and the shepherd's heart rejoices;
> so the Trojan fires shone....

I don't want to suggest that this translation is any better than Robert Fitzgerald's—I have the highest regard for his ability as a translator, and at the present time am reading his new translation of Vergil's *Aeneid* with great admiration—but I wanted to see what, if any, problems existed in the language itself. First I will discuss the two anomalies Mr. Lipking has pointed out and then I would like to answer his question about the function of the simile.

How can stars shine around the shining moon? Fitzgerald's use of the word "principal" in "principal stars" is not really ingenious. It is actually in the text. The adjective is ἀριπρεπέα [ἄστρα] (ariprepéa ástra), ἀριπρεπέα meaning in Greek "very distinguished" or "prominent." So Homer too, or whoever had coined the original simile, had noticed that even full moonshine allowed the more prominent stars to be visible.

There is no anomaly here.

But what about the second problem, the question that first bothered the Alexandrine scholars and still seems unresolved, namely, the problem of light breaking through *clouds* on a cloudless night. In the Greek, there are no clouds! Νήνεμος (némenos), which modifies αἰθήρ (aithér) specifically means "cloudless," as well as "still." So what happens to make a bright night become brighter? The Greek says ἄσπετος (áspetos)—"indescribably great" or "unspeakably great" air or sky or light ὑπερράγη (huper-rágei), "overflows" or "breaks out." What kind of light is this? What does it mean?

It seems to me that Homer is making a subjective observation rather than an objective one; possibly it is even a metaphysical observation. The scene is already bright because the moon is out, but all at once it becomes brighter. It is a trick of the eye. It is also a state of exaltation, and Pope was not so far wrong when he reinterpreted it as a religious spectacle because it reminded him of the shepherds who saw a supernatural light in the sky.

Fitzgerald's translation "as though pure space had broken through" seems to me quite wonderful, although it leaves out the idea of light, extraordinary light. The passage in Book XVI of the *Iliad*, which uses the same phrase, has been translated by another scholar as "and the boundless air of heaven breaks clear," which is closer to Homer, although less breathtaking than Fitzgerald's phrase. If there is a cloud that is being broken through here, it is in the minds of the Alexandrine scholars and all who followed them through the centuries, and not in the text. Pope's "A Flood of Glory bursts from all the Skies" is an inspired translation, even though it is a translation of meaning rather than language.

This image alone—a bright sky becoming brighter—illustrates the interesting possibilities of exploring the history of literary style. When Wordsworth adopts the image in his "A Night-Piece"—and I agree that something of his acquaintance with Pope's lines must have been in his mind when he wrote his own lines—the sequence becomes far more down-to-earth and reasonable (in this case, Wordsworth is reasonable and Pope is romantic, despite the fact that one would expect the reverse to be true).

Wordsworth's traveller looks up,

...and the clouds are split
Asunder,—and above his head he sees
The clear moon, and the glory of the heavens....

The scene is very natural and reasonable—the clouds part and the light appears. There is no supernatural epiphany as there is in Homer. The poet calls this a "Vision," but the traveller merely sees the moon breaking through.

We now come to the question Mr. Lipking first asked. I confess that as a practicing poet myself I am extremely interested in attempting to answer the question: What is Homer's simile *for*?

I believe that it serves both a dramatic and a psychological purpose. I see the poet as choreographer, one who directs the reader's (or listener's) attention, and who controls the reader's emotion. Before this passage appears, the reader's eyes have been riveted on the battle scene in the *Iliad*, with the Trojans driving the Greeks back to their ships. Our eyes have been on the earth, cast downward, like the eyes of Wordsworth's traveller. By raising the reader's eyes to Heaven, Homer changes the pace of the narrative. He goes into another gear, so to speak, and provides a kind of celestial relief to the bloody scenes that have just been enacted. This switch has the effect of giving a new, transcendent dimension not only to the specific scene, but to the whole event of the battle, and set beyond that, the whole war, and beyond that, the whole of man's heroic fate. What has happened to the reader or listener, when his attention is directed to the simile, is what has happened to Wordsworth's traveller: he had been looking down, eyes on the earth, but now he must look up and change his vision.

There are many such passages in Homer which, by the use of a sudden, transcendent simile, give dramatic relief and enlarge the meaning of the whole. Homer compels us to change our focus, our range of vision, both literally and figuratively. This is one of the ways—the actual technique and process—by which the simple account of a battle becomes a many-dimensional account of man's struggle in the universe. The function of the Homeric simile, as with our modern use of the metaphor, is to put the story into a larger perspective, to illuminate it so that it shines with an expanded vision.

The function of the event in Wordsworth is similar to what happens in Homer only on the first most obvious level: "a moment of calm and cheer snatched from the violence that surrounds it." But in Homer this level is also ironic. It forces the reader to see the pathos of the present by comparing the present to a more tranquil time. But the ultimate function of the simile is to set the heroic world in a larger context.

Like Wordsworth and Pope, every poet has the right to translate and select from his forerunners, although since the nineteenth century our scale has become even smaller and more intimate. Our literature has become far less heroic; it is often anti-heroic. But that is the subject for a separate discussion.

What I have done in these few minutes is illustrate exactly what Mr. Lipking has asserted: poets add and subtract dimensions of time and context from each other. To give a true account of this process, literary history must examine everything that concerns the poet: language, politics, history and society, the influence of foremothers and forefathers, but above all, the words themselves and their immediate and extended meanings. Only then can we hope to plumb some of the mysteries of poetic style.